CHRONOLOGY AND DOCUMENTARY
HANDBOOK OF THE
STATE OF
CALIFORNIA

ELLEN LLOYD TROVER,

State Editor

WILLIAM F. SWINDLER,

Series Editor

1972 OCEANA PUBLICATIONS, INC./ Dobbs Ferry, New York

This is Volume 5 in the series CHRONOLOGIES AND DOCUMENTARY HANDBOOKS OF THE STATES.

Library of Congress Cataloging in Publication Data
Main entry under title:

Chronology and documentary handbook of the State of
    California.

(Chronologies and documentary handbooks of the
States, v. 5)
SUMMARY: Contains a chronology of historical
events from 1540 to 1970, a directory of political
figures, an outline of the state constitution, and
copies of three historical documents.
    Bibliography: p.
    1. California--History--Chronology. 2. California
--Biography--Dictionaries. 3. California--History
--Sources. [1. California--History] I. Trover,
Ellen Lloyd, ed. II. Series.
F861.C5   979.4   72-5265
ISBN 0-379-16130-3

Manufactured in the United States of America

CONTENTS

INTRODUCTION

This projected series of *Chronologies and Documentary Handbooks of the States* will ultimately comprise fifty separate volumes – one for each of the states of the Union. Each volume is intended to provide a concise ready reference of basic data on the state, and to serve as a starting point for more extended study as the individual user may require. Hopefully, it will be a guidebook for a better informed citizenry – students, civic and service organizations, professional and business personnel, and others.

The editorial plan for the *Handbook* series falls into five divisions: (1) a chronology of selected events in the history of the state; (2) a short biographical directory of the principal public officials, e.g., governors, Senators and Representatives; (3) an analytical outline of the state constitution; (4) the text of some representative documents illustrating main currents in the political, economic, social or cultural history of the state; and (5) a selected bibliography for those seeking further or more detailed information. Most of the data found in the present volume, in fact, have been taken from one or another of these references.

The user of these *Handbooks* may ask why the full text of the state constitution, or the text of constitutional documents which affected the history of the state, have not been included. There are several reasons: In the case of the current constitution, the text in almost all cases is readily available from one or more official agencies within the state. In addition, the current constitutions of all fifty states, as well as the federal Constitution, are regularly kept up to date in the definitive collection maintained by the Legislative Drafting Research Fund of Columbia University and published by the publisher of the present series of *Handbooks*. These texts are available in most major libraries under the title, *Constitutions of the United States: National and State*, in two volumes, with a companion volume, the *Index Digest of State Constitutions*.

Finally, the complete collection of documents illustrative of the constitutional development of each state, from colonial or territorial status up to the current constitution as found in the Columbia University collection, is being prepared for publication in a multi-volume series by the present series editor. Whereas the present series of *Handbooks* is intended for a wide range of interested citizens, the series of annotated constitutional materials in the volumes of *Sources and Documents of U.S. Constitutions* is primarily for the specialist in government, history or law. This is not to suggest

v

that the general citizenry may not profit equally from referring to these materials; rather, it points up the separate purpose of the *Handbooks*, which is to guide the user to these and other sources of authoritative information with which he may systematically enrich his knowledge of this state and its place in the American Union.

William F. Swindler
Series Editor

vi

1540   On several occasions Hernando de Alarcon ascended the Colorado River and was probably the first white man to set foot in California.

October. Melchoir Diaz was sent from Coronado's expedition to contact Alarcon and touched California near where Alarcon did; he then traveled down the western bank of the Colorado.

1542   *September 28*. Juan Rodriguez Cabrillo discovered San Diego Bay which he named San Miguel; afterward he continued up the coast as far as Point Concepcion, returning to San Miguel Islands to die on January 3, 1543.

1579   *June 17*. Francis Drake's expedition landed, probably at the location now called Drake's Bay. Although Drake made perfunctory claim of area for England, and Spain eventually asserted claims as far north as modern Oregon, no attempt at systematic colonization of California was made for next 200 years.

1769   Under the direction of Jose de Galvez, four colonizing expeditions, two by sea and two by land, were sent to California. The commander-in-chief was Don Gaspar de Portola; and in charge of the spiritual phase was Father Junipero Serra.

July 16. Father Junipero Serra founded the mission of San Diego de Alcala; it was the first Catholic mission in California.

July 16. The Presidio of San Diego was founded.

November 1. The entrance to San Francisco Bay was discovered by Sergeant Jose de Ortega, pathfinder of Gaspar de Portola's expedition.

1770   *June 3*. The mission of San Carlos Borromeo and the presidio were formally established by Portola.

1771   *July 14.* The mission of San Antonio de Padua was
              founded.

              September 8. Mission San Gabriel Arcangel was
              founded on the direct overland route from Mexico to
              Monterey.

1772   *September 1.* The mission of San Luis Obispo de
              Tolosa was founded. Pueblo status was granted to the
              civilian community that grew up around the mission.

1773   *July.* Viceroy Bucareli issued a Reglamento providing
              government for Alta California, as part of the Spanish
              move towards greater attention to California.

1774   Juan Bautista de Anga led a company of colonists
              overland from Sonora by way of the Gila River and
              the Colorado Desert to San Gabriel and thence to
              Monterey.

              February 9. De Anza camped on the California bank
              of the Colorado.

1776   *September 17.* The Presidio of San Francisco was
              dedicated by 193 colonists led by Jose Joaquin
              Moraga.

              October 9. The mission of San Francisco de Asis was
              founded.

              Viceroy Bucareli instructed Felipe de Neve, Governor
              of the Californias, to transfer the seat of government
              to Monterey.

              November 1. The mission San Juan Capistrano was
              formally founded by Father Serra (it had been
              opened temporarily on October 30, 1775). Pueblo
              status was granted to the civilian community that
              grew up around the mission.

1777   *January 12.* The mission of Santa Clara de Asis was founded.

            August 28. The mission of Santa Cruz was founded.

            November 29. The pueblo of San Jose was founded.

1781   *September 4.* Founding of Los Angeles (El Pueblo de Nuestra Senora la Reina de los Angeles del Rio de Porciuncula); the official ceremony was not held until five years later.

1782   *March 31.* The Mission of San Buenaventura was established; it was the ninth and last mission founded by Father Serra.

            April 21. Santa Barbara, the last of the four presidial pueblos founded by the Spanish in Alta California, was established by Governor Felipe de Neve and Captain Jose Francisco Ortega, accompanied by Father Serra.

1784   *August 28.* Father Serra died.

1786   *September 14 - 24.* Comte de Laperouse on a round-the-world reconaissance voyage for France, stopped at Monterey; he was the first non-Spanish visitor to California since Drake.

            December 4. The Mission of Santa Barbara was founded.

1787   *December 8.* The Mission of La Purisima Concepcion was founded.

1790   The first Nootka treaty was signed between Spain and England, insuring the latter's presence in the Pacific northwest; George Vancouver was sent by Britain to see that the treaty was put into effect.

1791　　　　*August 28.* The Mission of Santa Cruz was founded.

　　　　　　October 9. The Mission of Nuestra Senora de la Soledad was founded.

1794　　　　Engineer Miguel Costanso advised that in addition to better presidios, California needed a second line of defense to which the presidials could back on in time of attack. Abortive attempts were made to find a location near San Francisco for a new town.

1796　　　　The first American ship entered a California port when the *Otter* under Ebenezer Dorr put out at Monterey for wood and water.

1797　　　　*June 11.* The Mission of San Jose de la Guadalupe was founded.

　　　　　　June 24. The Mission of San Juan Bautista was founded. Pueblo status was granted to the civilian community that grew up around the mission.

　　　　　　July 25. The Mission of San Miguel Arcangel was founded.

　　　　　　September 8. The Mission of San Fernando Rey de Espana was founded.

1798　　　　*June 13.* The Mission of San Luis Rey de Francia was founded.

1803　　　　The United States ship, the *Lelia Byrd*, entered the Bay of San Diego under the pretext of needing fresh food.

　　　　　　March 22. The bloodless Battle of San Diego occurred between the Spanish garrison and the fur traders on the *Lelia Byrd*.

1804　　　　*September 17.* The Mission of Santa Ones Virgin y Martin was founded.

1806   Count Nikolai Petrovich Rezonov secured temporary trading rights for the Russians in northern California.

            April 5. The *Juno* with Rezonov aboard entered San Francisco Bay.

1812   The Russian American Fur Company built the fortified village of Ross.

            September 10. Fort Ross (for *Rossia*, Russia) was formally dedicated.

1814   John Gilray, a British subject, became the first foreign resident in Spanish California after being sent ashore because of illness.

1817   *December 14*. The Mission of San Rafael Arcangel was founded.

1819   By the Treaty of 1819 with Spain the northern boarder was set at the 42nd parallel.

1822   News of Mexico's independence from Spain reached California.

1823   *July 4*. The Mission of San Francisco Solano was founded.

            Pueblo status was granted to the civilian community.

1824   The Russian government agreed to limit all future settlement to territory north of 54 degrees - 40 minutes.

            The Federal Constitution of the United Mexican States was adopted with California having the status of a territory.

1825   The first Governor of California under the Mexican regime arrived, Jose Maria Echeandia.

1826   *July 25.* Echeandia, the first Mexican governor, issued
            a decree authorizing married Indians of long standing
            Christianity to leave the missions. Eventually the
            friars were asked to take them back as they were
            unprepared to function in the secular world.

            Jedediah Strong Smith led the first American
            overland expedition to California.

1829   Echeandia published a Mexican law calling for the
            expulsion of all Spaniards, but he made no attempt to
            enforce it.

1834   *August 9.* Secularization of the missions was
            proclaimed by Governor Jose Figueroa, following
            orders from the Mexican Congress with half of the
            land to go to the Indians who were not empowered to
            dispose of their holdings.

1835   The Mexican Congress promoted Los Angeles from
            pueblo to ciudad (city) and ordered the capital
            transferred there.

1836   *November 7.* California was proclaimed a sovereign
            state after rebellion led by Juan Bautista Alvarado.

1840   Richard Henry Dana's *Two Years before the Mast* was
            published in the United States creating an interest in
            California.

1841   The United States increased its naval protection of
            the Pacific coast after a request for such protection
            from the American immigrants. For nearly twenty
            years American trappers had followed the rivers and
            mountain passes into the area, with occasional
            settlers following.

1842   *March.* Don Francisco Lopez found the first deposit
            of gold in commercial quantities at Placeritos Canyon
            (Los Angeles City).

1842   *October 19.* Commodore Thomas ap Catesby Jones of the United States seized Monterey on false information that the United States and Mexico were at war. He surrendered the town but it had caused great indignation in Mexico.

1845   *February 20 and 21.* The "Battle of Cahuenga Pass" was fought between the Mexican appointee to the civil and military government, Micheltorena, and his *chalos* and the forces of Alvarado and Castro. Although the casualties were only a horse on one side and a mule on the other, Micheltorena agreed to take his troops out of the province and Mexico lost its hold on California.

1846   The Donner Party was stranded on its way to settle in California, and perished of cannibalism and starvation.

      June. The Bear Flag Revolt led by Fremont occurred with the rebellion against the Mexican authority. Virtual breakdown of Mexican authority in California, and precarious position of American "squatters" in area, led to this unauthorized filibuster by group of adventurers.

      July 7. Commodore John D. Sloat became military governor after entering Monterey to forestall British intervention after the United States declared war on Mexico.

      July 23. Commodore Robert F. Stockton became military governor and extended United States control over southern California.

      August 15. The beginning of the weekly *Californian*, at Monterey the first newspaper in California, symbolized growing American dominance.

1847   *January 13.* The "Cahuenga Capitulation" was signed by Fremont and Andies Pico ending the Mexican War with respect to California.

1847   *January 19.* John C. Fremont claimed to be the
        military governor. A flamboyant adventurer, whose
        prowess was often exaggerated, Fremont's claim was
        disputed by his superior, General Stephen W. Kearny,
        who became military governor on March 1.

        May 31. Richard B. Mason became military governor.

1848   The original 28 counties were as follows: Los
        Angeles, San Diego, Santa Barbara, Butte, Colaveras,
        Colusa, El Dorado, Mariposa, Sacramento, San
        Joaquin, Shasta, Sutter, Tuolumme, Yolo, Yuba,
        Contra Costa, Marin, Mendocino, Monterey, Napa,
        San Francisco, San Luis Obispo, Santa Clara, Santa
        Cruz, Solano, Soneoma, Trinity, and San Diego.

        January 24. Gold was discovered in the foothills of
        the Sierra Nevada by James Marshall while
        constructing a sawmill at Coloma.

        February 2. The Treaty of Guadalupe Hidalgo was
        signed between Mexico and the United States with
        California being ceded to the United States officially.

        February 2 - September 9, 1850. Due to the crisis
        over slavery in the new territories, Congress provided
        no legal form of government.

        May 12. Samuel Brannan, leader of local Mormon
        colony, spread news of gold discoveries on American
        River to touch off business boom.

        August 7. Colonel Mason announced the formal
        cession to the United States and issued a code of
        Laws for the Better Government of California which,
        unfortunately, was not widely followed.

        November. The first Protestant congregation was
        formed in San Francisco; it was a union of sects in
        order to hire a minister.

1848   *December 5.* President Polk's official confirmation of gold discoveries in California touched off the great Gold Rush of 1849, overland and via Cape Horn. Within the year, nearly 40,000 persons had arrived to seek fortunes, and within next two years population rose to more than 100,000. Within four years of original discovery, more than $100,000,000 in gold had been mined.

    December 11. The citizens of San Jose considered "the propriety of establishing a Provisional Territorial Government for the protection of life and property." By the spring of 1849 most of California was considering the establishment of an independent government in the absence of territorial organization.

1849   Sacramento was settled on a portion of Sutter's grant.

    January. Peter H. Burnett presided over two meetings in Sacramento which discussed the necessity for government, still not officially established in the territory.

    February 12. A public meeting in Portsmouth Square created a "Legislative Assembly for the District of San Francisco."

    February 28. General Persifer F. Smith became military governor.

    April 13. General Bennett Riley became military governor.

    June. General Bennett Riley as governor issued a proclamation calling for a constitutional convention; he did so without authority but it placated the settlers, incensed at continued Congressional inaction on territorial organization.

    September 1. The constitutional convention met in Monterey which set the present boundaries of the

1849   state and wrote a constitution based on that of Iowa and New York's recent reforms.

                November 13. The first state officials were elected and the constitution was ratified (12,061 to 811).

                November 13. Peter H. Burnett, former judge of Oregon Territory, was elected governor, the first under the California constitution.

                December 15. The first legislature met in the first state capital, San Jose.

1850   *September 9.* The president signed the bill admitting California to the Union as the 31st state. Deadlock over extension of slavery into remaining territories had been chief cause of delay in action on California. Compromise of 1850 extended Missouri Compromise line to Pacific but excepted California, which was admitted as free state.

                Labor organizations began with the first printers' union in San Francisco.

                First census showed 92,597 population.

1851   *January 9.* John McDougal, Indiana Democrat, was inaugurated governor.

                Nevada County was formed from territory that had been originally a part of Yuba County; Nevada is Spanish for "snow-covered."

                Placu County was organized from parts of Sutter and Yuba counties.

                The College of the Pacific (Methodist) was chartered.

                March 3. Congress passed the bill for the establishment of a land commission to settle Spanish

1851   and Mexican claims. Over the years, sometimes arbitrary decisions of commission caused virtual disfranchisement of many claimants under Spanish and Mexican grants.

April 25. The United States government contracted with Absalom Woodward and George Charpenning for a monthly mail service between Salt Lake City and Sacramento.

June 9. The constitution for the first San Francisco "Committee of Vigilance" was adopted. Although described by their apologists as agencies of law and order, vigilantes were essentially lynch-oriented kangaroo courts.

1852   *January 8.* John Bigler, Democrat, was inaugurated governor.

Sierra County was organized from a part of Yuba County; it was named after the Sierra Nevada Mountains.

Siskiyou County was created from parts of Shasta and Klamath counties.

Tulare County (Spanish for "place of tules or rushes") was created.

January - March, 1856. The land commission held hearings; all its sessions were held in San Francisco except for one brief term at Los Angeles. More than 800 claims were brought before it and 604 of them, involving nearly 9,000,000 acres, were confirmed.

1853   Alameda County was created. The primary meaning of the word *alameda* is "a place where poplar trees grow."

Humboldt County was organized; it was named for the German scientist and traveler, Baron Alexander von Humboldt.

1853 San Bernardino County (named for St. Bernard) was organized from territory which was at first part of Los Angeles and San Diego counties.

1854 Amador County was created; it was named after Jose Maria Amador, a miner in that region in 1848 and previously major-domo of the Mission San Jose.

 Stanislaus County was organized from a part of Tuolumme County.

 Plumas County was organized from a portion of Butte County; the name was derived from El Rio de las Plumas, "the river of the feathers," so named by Captain Luis A. Arguello, who led an exploring party up the valley of the Feather River in 1820.

 In *People v. Hall* the state supreme court extended the constitutional ban on testimony against a white by an Indian to exclude the Chinese as well since "Indian" was interpreted as a generic term intended to cover all nonwhites.

1855 Merced County was organized from a part of Mariposa County; it was named from the river which Gabriel Moraga, in 1806, had called El Rio de Nuestra Senora de la Merced, "The River of Our Lady of Mercy."

 The College of California in Oakland was chartered to a group of new England Congregationalists and Presbyterians; in 1868 the state took over the college which became the University of California.

1856 *January 9.* J. Neely Johnson, candidate of American or "Know-Nothing" party, became governor.

 Fresno County was created.

 San Mateo County was organized, being formed from the southern portion of San Francisco County.

1856   Tehama County was organized from parts of Colusa,
            Butte, and Shasta counties.

            May 14. The second vigilance committee in San
            Francisco was organized.

1857   Del Norte County (Spanish for "of the north") was
            organized.

            The first commercial orange grove was planted by
            William Wolfskill near the pueblo of Los Angeles.

            August 9. A mail service was established between San
            Diego and San Antonio, Texas.

1858   *January 8*. John B. Weller, Democrat, became
            governor.

1859   The legislature approved a plan that the part of
            California south of 35 degrees-45 minutes (the
            northern boundary of San Luis Obispo County)
            should become the territory of Colorado. The voters
            of the region approved the plan, but Congress did
            not.

1860   *January 9*. Milton S. Latham became governor until
            his appointment to the United States Senate.

            January 9. John G. Downey became governor. He was
            the only naturalized governor and the first from
            southern California.

            April. The Pony Express began to serve San
            Francisco.

            Population: 379,994.

1861   Mono County was formed from territory taken from
            Calaveras and Fresno counties.

1861   California's first oil well was drilled near Eureka.

              George S. Gilbert built a small refinery on the Ojai
              Ranch north of Ventura; from seepage oil, he
              produced small quantities of kerosene.

              May 2. Lake County was set off from Napa County.

1862   *January 10.* Leland Stanford, Republican, became
              governor. A railroad magnate, he subsequently was
              elected to U.S. Senate.

              July 1. President Lincoln signed a bill entitled "An
              act to aid in the construction of a railroad and
              telegraph line from the Missouri River to the Pacific
              Ocean."

1863   *January 8.* Construction was begun on the Central
              Pacific Railway from Sacramento.

              December 10. Frederick F. Low, Union party,
              became the first four-year-term governor.

1864   Lassen County was organized from parts of Plumas
              and Shasta counties; it was named for pioneer Peter
              Lassen.

              March 16. Alpine County was created from parts of
              El Dorado, Calaveras, Tuolumme, and Amador
              counties.

1866   Inyo County ("dwelling place of the great spirit") was
              organized from territory that had been set aside two
              years earlier from Mono and Tulare counties and
              called Coso County. However, Coso County was
              never organized and Inyo took its place.

              Kern County was organized from parts of Los
              Angeles and Tulare counties; it was named after the
              Kern River which Fremont named in honor of

1866   Edward M. Kern, topographer of the expedition of 1845-1846.

1867   *December 5*. Henry H. Haight, Democrat, became governor.

1868   The government granted Wells Fargo a yearly subsidy for a daily mail service to California.

            March 23. The University of California was established by the state legislature.

1869   *May 10*. The Central Pacific Railway joined the Union Pacific in Promontory, Utah, linking California to the east.

1870   The separate but equal rationale of schools was excepted when a Negro couple tried to enroll their child in a white school and the *Ward v. Flood* decision stopped them.

            Population: 560,247.

1871   *December 8*. Newton Booth, Republican, became governor until he left for the United States Senate.

1872   Ventura County was organized; its name is a corruption of San Buenaventura.

1874   Fresno County (Spanish for "ash tree") was organized.

            San Benito County was formed from a part of Monterey County; it derived its name from San Benito Creek which was named by Father Crespi in 1772.

            Modoc County was formed from a part of Siskiyou County.

1875   *March 4.* Romualdo Pacheco, Republican, became
            governor. He was the first native-born governor.

            December 9. William Irwin, Democrat, became
            governor.

1877   *September 5.* The voters approved a measure for a
            new state constitutional convention.

1878   *September 28.* The constitutional convention met at
            Sacramento.

1879   *May 17.* The constitution was adopted by a majority
            of less than 11,000 out of a total vote of 145,000.

1880   *January 8.* George C. Perkins was inaugurated
            governor, the only one ever elected to a three-year
            term.

            April 15. The State Board of Railroad Commissioners
            was established by the legislature to regulate rates and
            examine accounts.

            Population: 864,694.

1882   Federal law placed a ban on Chinese immigration for
            ten years; in 1892 this was extended for another ten
            years; and in 1902 the ban became permanent.

1883   *January 10.* George Stoneman was inaugurated
            governor.

1887   *January 8.* Washington Bartlett was inaugurated
            governor and served until his death on September 12.

            September 13. Robert W. Waterman was inaugurated
            governor.

1889   Orange County was created from a portion of Los
            Angeles County.

1890   Population: 1,213,398.

1891   *January 8*. Henry H. Markham was inaugurated governor.

                Glenn County was organized when it was separated from Colusa County; it was named in honor of Dr. Hugh James Glenn, a prominent rancher.

1892   John Muir led in founding the Sierra Club dedicated to protecting the Yosemite and Sierra wildernesses.

1893   Madera County ("wood" in Spanish) was organized from a part of Fresno County.

                Kings County was organized from territory set off from Tulare County; it was named for the river called El Rio de los Santos Reyes, "River of the Holy Kings", in honor of the Three Wise Men by a Spanish explorer, probably Gabriel Moraga in 1805.

                Riverside County was created from territory originally belonging to San Bernardino and San Diego counties.

1895   *January 11*. James H. Budd, Democrat, became governor.

1899   *January 4*. Henry T. Gage, Republican, became governor.

                April. Work was begun on the breakwater at San Pedro to protect Los Angeles Harbor.

1900   Population: 1,485,053.

1903   *January 7*. George C. Pardee, Republican, became governor.

1905   The Colorado River burst into the Imperial Canal and created the Salton Sea before it was checked in 1907.

1906   *April 18.* The great San Francisco earthquake and fires occurred when the San Andreas Fault shifted.

The San Francisco school board announced that Oriental students would be segregated; President Roosevelt intervened and the order was rescinded only to be reissued later in the year.

1907   *January 9.* James N. Gillett, Republican, became governor.

Imperial County was organized from that part of San Diego County known as Imperial Valley.

1908   Construction began on the Owens Valley acqueduct to bring water to the city of Los Angeles.

1909   Supplementary legislation to the 1908 constitutional amendment made popular vote mandatory to select party nominees.

1910   Population: 2,377,549.

1911   *January 3.* Hiram W. Johnson, Republican, became governor. He was the first four-year governor to be re-elected and served until he left for the United States Senate.

California acquired the most comprehensive system of public utility regulation then in existence.

1913   The Weld Act or the Alien Land Law was passed; under it, aliens ineligible for citizenship could not acquire land or lease it for over three years. President Wilson had tried unsuccessfully to stop its passage.

1917   *March 15.* William D. Stephens, Republican, became governor.

1919   The state organization of the Communist party was formed at a convention in Oakland.

1919   *April*. The legislature passed a criminal syndicalism
                act; a criminal syndicalism was "any doctrine or
                precept advocating ... unlawful acts of force and
                violence ... as a means of accomplishing a change in
                industrial ownership or control, or effecting any
                political change."

1920   Population: 3,426,861.

1923   *January 9*. Friend W. Richardson, Republican,
                became governor.

1926   Two plans for amendment to the constitution were
                put before the electorate: the "Los Angeles plan"
                called for reapportionment according to population
                in both houses and delegation to a commission of ex
                officio members with power to act if the legislature
                failed; and the "Federal plan" apportioning seats in
                the lower house by population and in the upper
                house by county. The voters chose the Federal plan.

1927   *January 4*. Clement C. Young, Republican, became
                governor.

1930   Population: 5,677,251.

1931   *1931 - June 2, 1934*. James Rolph, Jr., Republican,
                was governor; he collapsed and died during a
                precampaign tour.

1933   A 1% sales tax was passed by the legislature to
                provide school funds but the governor vetoed an
                income tax measure.

1934   *June 2*. Frank F. Merriam, Republican, became
                governor; he had been Lieutenant-Governor under
                James Rolph, Jr.

1939   *January 2*. Culbert L. Olson, Democrat, became
                governor.

1940   Population: 6,907,387.

1941   The legislature created the Tenney Committee which
              lasted until 1949 in its function of exposing the
              Communist menace. It was finally ended when
              Tenney attacked respected legislators.

              The Colorado River Aqueduct was completed,
              bringing water to the coastal cities from the
              Colorado.

1942   Under an act of Congress and an agreement with
              Mexico, the United States Department of Agriculture
              assumed the responsibility for the care of temporary
              immigrant workers from Mexico.

1943   *January 4*. Earl Warren, Republican, became
              governor. He has been the only three-term governor
              to date.

1948   The Board of Supervisors of Los Angeles ordered that
              all Communist books be removed from the county
              library. The supervisors relented after strong public
              protest.

1950   *April*. The state Appellate Court invoked the United
              Nations Charter to void the 1920 alien land law
              barring ownership by Asiatics; this was the first use of
              the Charter as a principle for a ruling by a United
              States Court.

              October. The legislature passed Governor Warren's
              proposed bill requiring all public employees of the
              state to sign an oath swearing non-membership in any
              organization pledged to overthrow the government,
              non-membership in the past five years and during
              post tenure. (Levering Act).

              Population: 10,586,223.

1951   *April.* The Third District Court ruled the special university loyalty oath was a violation of tenure and unconstitutional.

1952   Cesar Chavez began to unionize migratory farm workers when he went to work for the AFL-CIO, Community Service Organization.

The State Supreme Court finally ruled the Weld Act (Alien Land Law) unconstitutional.

October. The California Supreme Court, 6-1, upheld the constitutionality of the Levering Act requiring public employees to take loyalty oath.

October. On the same day the Levering Act was upheld, the State Supreme Court held the 1949 act requiring loyalty oaths only of university faculty was invalid (*Tolman v. California*).

November. The voters incorporated the Levering Act into the constitution.

1953   *October 4.* Goodwin J. Knight, Republican, became governor; he had been Lieutenant Governor under Warren who left to become Chief Justice of the United States.

1954   *June.* Indians claimed 75 million of the state's 103 million acres before the Federal Claims Commission.

1956   *December.* A group of citizens from 8 northern counties urged Representative Engle to offer a bill to make a new state of those counties (Shasta) due to alleged aggression of southern California over water plans.

1959   *January 5.* Edmund G. Brown, Democrat, became governor.

1959   *February.* The Nevada Assembly passed a bill
              claiming a 40,000 square mile area of California; the
              last tract had been in dispute since 1861; the
              California legislature treated the bill as a joke.

1960   *March.* The United States Supreme Court upheld the
              law letting state or local governments oust employees
              who refused to answer queries by state or Federal
              investigative bodies on alleged subversive activities.

              Population: 15,717,204.

1962   Cesar Chavez began an independent farm labor union,
              the national Farm Workers Association which had
              50,000 members by August, 1964.

1963   *August.* Governor Brown signed an executive order
              setting up fair practices code aimed at ending all
              racial and religious discrimination; a civil rights task
              force was set up to police compliance.

1964   *November and December.* The University of
              California at Berkeley had student riots following
              university rule forbidding political activities on
              campus.

1965   *August.* The Watts Riots by Negroes in Los Angeles
              took place. The toll of the riots was: 34 dead, 1,032
              injured, 3,952 arrested, 3,411 charged with felony or
              misdemeanor and $40,000,000 property damage.

1966   The legislature enacted a tough law on
              conflict-of-interest aimed at state officers.

1967   *January 5.* Ronald Reagan, Republican, became
              governor.

              December 21. The State Supreme Court declared the
              Levering loyalty oath to be an infringement of First
              Amendment rights and therefore invalid.

1969   *September.* The State Supreme Court narrowed the
            application of capital punishment by tightening the
            definition of kidnapping under the "Little Lindbergh
            Act." In December, 1967, the court had come within
            one vote of abolishing the death penalty.

1970   *February 11.* The 1968 suit by the ACLU against the
            Los Angeles Board of Education for school
            segregation was settled when the court ruled there
            was segregation de jure violating state and federal
            law. Pending appeal, President Nixon issued a white
            paper on March 24, criticizing the holding.

BIOGRAPHICAL DIRECTORY

Governors of the Spanish Period

Gaspar de Portola, 1768-70
Pedro Foges, 1770-73, 1782-91
Fernando Rivera y Moncada, 1773-75
Felipe de Neve, 1775-82
Jose Antonio Romeu, 1791-92
Jose J. de Arrillaga, 1792-94, 1800-14
Diego de Borica, 1794-1800
Jose Arguello, 1814-15
Pablo Vicente de Sola, 1815-22
Luis Arguello, 1822-25

Governors of the Mexican Period

Jose Maria Echeandia, 1825-31
Manuel Victoria, 1831-32
Pio Pico, Jose Maria Echeandia,
Agustin V. Zamorano (regional governors,
1832-33)
Jose Figueroa, 1833-35
Jose Castro, 1835-36
Nicolas Gutierrez, Mariano Chico, Juan
Bautista Alvarado, 1836-41
Manuel Micheltorena, 1841-45
Pio Pico, 1845-46
Jose Maria Flores, 1846-47

Military Governors

John D. Sloat, Robert F. Stockton, John
C. Fremont, Stephen W. Kearny, Richard
B. Mason, 1847-49

AXTELL, Samuel B.
  b. Oct. 14, 1819, Columbus, O.
  d. Aug. 6, 1891, Morristown, N.J.
  U. S. Representative, 1869-71
BARBOUR, Henry E.
  b. Mar. 8, 1877, Ogdensburg, N.Y.
  d. Mar. 21, 1945, Fresno, Calif.
  U. S. Representative, 1919-33
BARD, Thomas R.
  b. Dec. 8, 1841, Chambersburg, Pa.
  d. Mar. 5, 1915, Ventura County, Calif.
  U. S. Senator, 1900-05
BARHAM, John A.
  b. July 17, 1843, Cass County, Mo.
  d. Jan. 22, 1926, Santa Rosa, Calif.
  U. S. Representative, 1895-1901
BARLOW, Charles A.
  b. Mar. 17, 1858, Cleveland, O.
  d. Oct. 3, 1927, Bakersfield, Calif.
  U. S. Representative, 1897-99
BARTLETT, Washington
  b. Feb. 29, 1824, Savannah, Ga.
  d. Sept. 12, 1887, San Francisco, Calif.
  Governor, 1887
BELL, Charles W.
  b. June 11, 1857, Albany, N.Y.
  d. Apr. 19, 1927, Pasadena, Calif.
  U. S. Representative, 1913-15
BELL, Theodore A.
  b. July 25, 1872, Vallejo, Calif.
  d. Sept. 4, 1922, San Rafael, Calif.
  U. S. Representative, 1903-05
BENEDICT, H. Stanley
  b. Feb. 20, 1878, Boonville, Mo.
  d. July 10, 1930, London, England
  U. S. Representative, 1916-17
BERRY, Campbell P.
  b. Nov. 7, 1834, Jackson County, Ala.
  d. Jan. 8, 1901, Wheatland, Calif.
  U. S. Representative, 1879-83

BIDWELL, John
  b. Aug. 5, 1819, Chautauqua, N.Y.
  d. Apr. 4, 1900, Chico, Calif.
  U. S. Representative, 1865-67
BIGGS, Marion
  b. May 2, 1823, Curryville, Mo.
  d. Aug. 2, 1910, Sacramento, Calif.
  U. S. Representative, 1887-91
BIGLER, John
  b. Jan. 8, 1805, Carlisle, Pa.
  d. Nov. 29, 1871, in California
  Governor, 1852-56
BOOTH, Newton
  b. Dec. 25, 1825, Salem, Ind.
  d. July 14, 1892, Sacramento, Calif.
  Governor, 1871-75
  U. S. Senator, 1875-81
BOWERS, William W.
  b. Oct. 20, 1834, Whitestown, N.Y.
  d. May 2, 1917, San Diego, Calif.
  U. S. Representative, 1891-97
BRADLEY, Willis W.
  b. June 28, 1884, Niagara County, N.Y.
  d. Aug. 27, 1954, Santa Barbara, Calif.
  U. S. Representative, 1947-49
BRODERICK, David C.
  b. Feb. 4, 1820, Washington, D. C.
  d. Sept. 16, 1859, San Francisco, Calif.
  U. S. Senator, 1857-59
BUCK, Frank H.
  b. Sept. 23, 1887, Solano County, Calif.
  d. Sept. 17, 1942, Washington, D. C.
  U. S. Representative, 1933-42
BUDD, James H.
  b. May 18, 1851, Janesville, Wisc.
  d. July 30, 1908, Stockton, Calif.
  Governor, 1894-98
BURCH, John C.
  b. Feb. 1, 1826, Boone County, Mo.
  d. Aug. 31, 1885, San Francisco, Calif.
  U. S. Representative, 1859-61

BURKE, John H.
  b. June 2, 1894, Excelsior, Wisc.
  d. May 14, 1951, Long Beach, Calif.
  U. S. Representative, 1933-35
BURNETT, Peter H.
  b. Nov. 15, 1807, Nashville, Tenn.
  d. May 17, 1895, San Francisco, Calif.
  Governor, 1849-50
BURNHAM, George
  b. Dec. 28, 1868, London, England
  d. June 28, 1939, San Diego, Calif.
  U. S. Representative, 1933-37
CAMINETTI, Anthony
  b. July 30, 1854, Jackson, Calif.
  d. Nov. 17, 1923, Jackson, Calif.
  U. S. Representative, 1891-95
CANNON, Marion
  b. Oct. 30, 1834, Morgantown, W. Va.
  d. Aug. 27, 1920, Ventura, Calif.
  U. S. Representative. 1893-95
CASSERLY, Eugene
  b. Nov. 13, 1820, in Ireland
  d. June 14, 1883, San Francisco, Calif.
  U. S. Senator, 1869-73
CASTLE, Curtis H.
  b. Oct. 4, 1848, Knox County, Ill.
  d. July 21, 1928, Santa Barbara, Calif.
  U. S. Representative, 1897-99
CHURCH, Denver S.
  b. Dec. 11, 1862, Folsom City, Calif.
  d. Feb. 21, 1952, Fresno, Calif.
  U. S. Representative, 1913-19, 1933-35
CLAYTON, Charles
  b. Oct. 5, 1825, Devonshire, England
  d. Oct. 4, 1885, Oakland, Calif.
  U. S. Representative, 1873-75
CLUNIE, Thomas J.
  b. Mar. 25, 1852, St. Johns, Nfld.
  d. June 30, 1903, San Francisco, Calif.
  U. S. Representative, 1889-91

COGHLAN, John M.
  b. Dec. 8, 1835, Louisville, Ky.
  d. Mar. 26, 1879, Oakland, Calif.
  U. S. Representative, 1871-73
COLDEN, Charles C.
  b. Aug. 24, 1870, Peoria County, Ill.
  d. Apr. 15, 1938, Washington, D. C.
  U. S. Representative, 1933-38
COLE, Cornelius
  b. Sept. 17, 1822, Seneca County, N.Y.
  d. Nov. 3, 1924, Hollywood, Calif.
  U. S. Representative, 1863-65
  U. S. Senator, 1867-73
CONNESS, John
  b. Sept. 22, 1821, in Ireland
  d. Jan. 10, 1909, Jamaica Plain, N.Y.
  U. S. Senator, 1863-69
COOMBS, Frederick L.
  b. Dec. 27, 1853, Napa, Calif.
  d. Oct. 5, 1934, Napa, Calif.
  U. S. Representative, 1901-03
CRAIL, Joe
  b. Dec. 25, 1877, Fairfield, Ia.
  d. Mar. 2, 1938, Los Angeles, Calif.
  U. S. Representative, 1927-33
CURRY, Charles F.
  b. Mar. 14, 1858, Naperville, Ill.
  d. Oct. 10, 1930, Washington, D. C.
  U. S. Representative, 1913-30
CUTTING, John T.
  b. Sept. 7, 1844, Westport, N.Y.
  d. Nov. 24, 1911, Toronto, Can.
  U. S. Representative, 1891-93
DANIELS, Milton J.
  b. Apr. 18, 1838, Cobleskill, N.Y.
  d. Dec. 1, 1914, Riverside, Calif.
  U. S. Representative, 1903-05
DAVIS, Horace
  b. Mar. 16, 1831, Worcester, Mass.
  d. July 12, 1916, San Francisco, Calif.
  U. S. Representative, 1877-81

DeHAVEN, John J.
  b. Mar. 12, 1849, St. Joseph, Mo.
  d. Jan. 26, 1913, Yountville, Calif.
  U. S. Representative, 1889-90
DENVER, James W.
  b. Oct. 23, 1817, Winchester, Va.
  d. Aug. 9, 1892, Washington, D. C.
  U. S. Representative, 1855-57
  Governor, Kansas Territory, 1857-58
DeVRIES, Marion
  b. Aug. 15, 1865, San Joaquin County, Calif.
  d. Sept. 11, 1939, Woodbridge, Calif.
  U. S. Representative, 1897-1900
DOCKWEILER, John F.
  b. Sept. 19, 1895, Los Angeles, Calif.
  d. Jan. 31, 1943, Los Angeles, Calif.
  U. S. Representative, 1933-39
DOWNEY, Sheridan
  b. Mar. 11, 1884, Laramie, Wyo.
  d. Oct. 25, 1961, San Francisco, Calif.
  U. S. Senator, 1939-50
EATON, Thomas M.
  b. Aug. 3, 1896, Madison County, Ill.
  d. Sept. 16, 1939, Long Beach, Calif.
  U. S. Representative, 1939
ELLIOTT, James T.
  b. Apr. 22, 1823, Columbus, Ga.
  d. July 28, 1875, Camden, Ark.
  U. S. Representative, 1867-69
ELSTON, John A.
  b. Feb. 10, 1874, Woodland, Calif.
  d. Dec. 15, 1921, Washington, D. C.
  U. S. Representative, 1915-21
ENGLEBRIGHT, Harry L.
  b. Jan. 2, 1884, Nevada City, Calif.
  d. May 13, 1943, Bethesda, Md.
  U. S. Representative, 1926-43
ENGLEBRIGHT, William F.
  b. Nov. 23, 1855, New Bedford, Mass.
  d. Feb. 10, 1915, Oakland, Calif.
  U. S. Representative, 1907-11

ENGLISH, Warren B.
  b. May 1, 1840, Charleston, W. Va.
  d. Jan. 9, 1913, Santa Rosa, Calif.
  U. S. Representative, 1894-95
EVANS, William E.
  b. Dec. 14, 1877, Laurel County, Ky.
  d. Nov. 12, 1959, Los Angeles, Calif.
  U. S. Representative, 1927-35
FARLEY, James T.
  b. Aug. 6, 1829, Albemarle County, Va.
  d. Jan. 22, 1886, Jackson, Calif.
  U. S. Senator, 1879-85
FELTON, Charles N.
  b. Jan. 1, 1828, Buffalo, N. Y.
  d. Sept. 13, 1914, Menlo Park, Calif.
  U. S. Representative, 1885-89
  U. S. Senator, 1891-93
FLAHERTY, Lawrence J.
  b. July 4, 1878, San Mateo, Calif.
  d. June 13, 1926, New York, N. Y.
  U. S. Representative, 1925-26
FLINT, Frank P.
  b. July 15, 1862, N. Reading, Mass.
  d. Feb. 11, 1929, in Phillipines
  U. S. Senator, 1905-11
FORD, Thomas F.
  b. Feb. 18, 1873, St. Louis, Mo.
  d. Dec. 26, 1958, S. Pasadena, Calif.
  U. S. Representative, 1933-45
FREDERICKS, John D.
  b. Sept. 10, 1869, Gurgettstown, Pa.
  d. Aug. 26, 1945, Los Angeles, Calif.
  U. S. Representative, 1923-27
FREE, Arthur M.
  b. Jan. 15, 1879, San Jose, Calif.
  d. Apr. 1, 1953, San Jose, Calif.
  U. S. Representative, 1921-33
FREMONT, John C.
  b. Jan. 21, 1813, Savannah, Ga.
  d. July 13, 1890, New York, N.Y.
  Military governor, 1849
  U. S. Senator, 1850-51

GAGE, Henry T.
  b. Nov. 25, 1852, Geneva, N.Y.
  d. Aug. 28, 1924, in California
  Governor, 1899-1903
GEARHART, Bertrand W.
  b. May 31, 1890, Fresno, Calif.
  d. Oct. 11, 1955, Fresno, Calif.
  U. S. Representative, 1935-49
GEARY, Thomas J.
  b. Jan. 18, 1854, Boston, Mass.
  d. July 6, 1929, Santa Rosa, Calif.
  U. S. Representative, 1890-95
GEYER, Lee E.
  b. Sept. 9, 1888, Wetmore, Kan.
  d. Oct. 11, 1941, Washington, D.C.
  U. S. Representative, 1939-41
GILBERT, Edward
  b. 1819 in Cherry Valley, N.Y.
  d. Aug. 2, 1852, Sacramento, Calif.
  U. S. Representative, 1850-51
GILLETT, James N.
  b. Sept. 20, 1860, Viroqua, Wisc.
  d. Aug. 20, 1937, Berkeley, Calif.
  U. S. Representative, 1903-06
  Governor, 1907-11
GLASCOCK, John R.
  b. Aug. 25, 1845, Panola County, Miss.
  d. Nov. 10, 1913, Woodside, Calif.
  U. S. Representative, 1883-85
GWIN, William C.
  b. Oct. 9, 1805, Sumner County, Tenn.
  d. Sept. 3, 1885, New York, N. Y.
  U. S. Representative (Miss.), 1841-43
  U. S. Senator, 1850-61
HAGER, John S.
  b. Mar. 12, 1818, Morris County, N.J.
  d. Mar. 19, 1890, San Francisco, Calif.
  U. S. Senator, 1874-75
HAIGHT, Henry H.
  b. May 20, 1825, Rochester, N. Y.
  d. Sept. 2, 1878, San Francisco, Calif.
  Governor, 1867-71

HAUN, Henry P.
  b. Jan. 18, 1815, Newtown, Ky.
  d. June 6, 1860, Marysville, Calif.
  U. S. Senator, 1859-60
HAYES, Everis A.
  b. Mar. 10, 1855, Waterloo, Wisc.
  d. June 3, 1942, San Jose, Calif.
  U. S. Representative, 1905-19
HEARST, George
  b. Sept. 3, 1820, Sullivan, Mo.
  d. Feb. 28, 1891, Washington, D.C.
  U. S. Senator, 1886, 1887-91
HENLEY, Barclay
  b. Mar. 17, 1843, Charlestown, Ind.
  d. Feb. 15, 1914, San Francisco, Calif.
  U. S. Representative, 1883-87
HERBERT, Philemon T.
  b. Nov. 1, 1825, Pine Apple, Ala.
  d. July 23, 1864, Kingston, La.
  U. S. Representative, 1855-57
HERSMAN, Hugh S.
  b. July 8, 1872, Port Deposit, Md.
  d. Mar. 7, 1954, San Francisco, Calif.
  U. S. Representative, 1919-21
HIGBY, William
  b. Aug. 18, 1813, Willsboro, N.Y.
  d. Nov. 27, 1887, Santa Rosa, Calif.
  U. S. Representative, 1863-67
HILBORN, Samuel G.
  b. Dec. 9, 1834, Minot, Me.
  d. Apr. 19, 1899, Washington, D.C.
  U. S. Representative, 1892-99
HINSHAW, J. Carl
  b. July 28, 1894, Chicago, Ill.
  d. Aug. 25, 1956, Bethesda, Md.
  U. S. Representative, 1939-56
HOUGHTON, Sherman O.
  b. Apr. 10, 1828, New York, N.Y.
  d. Aug. 31, 1914, Los Angeles, Calif.
  U. S. Representative, 1871-75

IRWIN, William
  b. 1827, in Ohio
  d. Mar. 15, 1886, San Francisco, Calif.
  Governor, 1875-79
JOHNSON, Grove L.
  b. Mar. 27, 1841, Syracuse, N.Y.
  d. Feb. 1, 1926, Sacramento, Calif.
  U. S. Representative, 1895-97
JOHNSON, Hiram W.
  b. Sept. 2, 1866, Sacramento, Calif.
  d. Aug. 6, 1945, Bethesda, Md.
  Governor, 1911-17
  U. S. Senator, 1917-45
JOHNSON, James A.
  b. May 16, 1829, Spartansburg, S.C.
  d. May 11, 1896, San Francisco, Calif.
  U. S. Representative, 1869-71
JOHNSON, J. Leroy
  b. Apr. 8, 1888, Wausau, Wisc.
  d. Mar. 26, 1961, Stockton, Calif.
  U. S. Representative, 1943-57
JOHNSON, J. Neely
  b. 1828, in Indiana
  d. August 1872, Salt Lake City, Utah
  Governor, 1856-58
KAHN, Florence P.
  b. Nov. 9, 1868, Salt Lake City, Utah
  d. Nov. 16, 1948, San Francisco, Calif.
  U. S. Representative, 1925-37
KAHN, Julius
  b. Feb. 28, 1861, in Germany
  d. Dec. 18, 1924, San Francisco, Calif.
  U. S. Representative, 1899-1903, 1905-24
KENT, William
  b. Mar. 29, 1864, Chicago, Ill.
  d. Mar. 13, 1928, Kentfield, Calif.
  U. S. Representative, 1911-17
KETTNER, William
  b. Nov. 20, 1864, Ann Arbor, Mich.
  d. Nov. 11, 1930, San Diego, Calif.
  U. S. Representative, 1913-21

KRAMER, Charles
  b. Apr. 18, 1879, Paducah, Ky.
  d. Jan. 20, 1943, Los Angeles, Calif.
  U. S. Representative, 1933-43
LATHAM, Milton S.
  b. May 23, 1827, Columbus, O.
  d. Mar. 4, 1882, New York, N.Y.
  U. S. Representative, 1853-55
  U. S. Senator, 1860-63
LINEBERGER, Walter F.
  b. July 20, 1883, Hardeman County, Tenn.
  d. Oct. 9, 1943, Santa Barbara, Calif.
  U. S. Representative, 1921-27
LIVERNASH, Edward J.
  b. Feb. 14, 1866, San Andreas, Calif.
  d. June 1, 1938, Agnew, Calif.
  U. S. Representative, 1903-04
LOUD, Eugene F.
  b. Mar. 12, 1847, Abingdon, Mass.
  d. Dec. 19, 1908, San Francisco, Calif.
  U. S. Representative, 1891-1903
LOUTTIT, James A.
  b. Oct. 16, 1848, New Orleans, La.
  d. July 26, 1908, Pacific Grove, Calif.
  U. S. Representative, 1885-87
LOW, Frederick F.
  b. July 20, 1828, Franklin, Me.
  d. July 21, 1894, San Francisco, Calif.
  U. S. Representative, 1861-63
  Governor, 1863-67
LUTTRELL, John K.
  b. June 27, 1831, Knox County, Tenn.
  d. Oct. 4, 1893, Sitka, Alaska
  U. S. Representative, 1873-79
McADOO, William Gibbs
  b. Oct. 31, 1863, Cobb County, Ga.
  d. Feb. 1, 1941, Washington, D. C.
  U. S. Senator, 1933-38
McCORKLE, Joseph W.
  b. June 24, 1819, Piqua, O.
  d. Mar. 18, 1884, Branchville, Md.
  U. S. Representative, 1851-53

McDOUGALL, James A.
  b. Nov. 19, 1817, Bethlehem, N.Y.
  d. Sept. 3, 1867, Albany, N.Y.
  U. S. Representative, 1853-55
  U. S. Senator, 1861-67
McDOUGALL, John
  b. 1818, in Ohio
  d. Mar. 30, 1866, San Francisco, Calif.
  Governor, 1851-52
McGRATH, John J.
  b. July 23, 1877, in Ireland
  d. Aug. 25, 1951, San Mateo, Calif.
  U. S. Representative, 1933-39
McGROARTY, John S.
  b. Aug. 20, 1862, Luzerne County, Pa.
  d. Aug. 7, 1944, Los Angeles, Calif.
  U. S. Representative, 1935-39
McKENNA, Joseph
  b. Aug. 10, 1843, Philadelphia, Pa.
  d. Nov. 21, 1926, Washington, D.C.
  U. S. Representative, 1885-92
  U. S. Supreme Court, 1892-1925
McKIBBIN, Joseph C.
  b. May 14, 1824, Chambersburg, Pa.
  d. July 1, 1896, Washington, D.C.
  U. S. Representative, 1857-59
McKINLEY, Duncan E.
  b. Oct. 6, 1862, Orillia, Can.
  d. Dec. 30, 1914, Berkeley, Calif.
  U. S. Representative, 1905-11
McLACHLAN, James
  b. Aug. 1, 1852, in Scotland
  d. Nov. 21, 1940, Los Angeles, Calif.
  U. S. Representative, 1895-97, 1901-11
MacLAFFERTY, James H.
  b. Feb. 27, 1871, San Diego, Calif.
  d. June 9, 1937, Oakland, Calif.
  U. S. Representative, 1921-25
McRUER, Donald C.
  b. Mar. 10, 1826, Bangor, Me.
  d. Jan. 29, 1898, St. Helena, Calif.
  U. S. Representative, 1865-67

MAGUIRE, James G.
  b. Feb. 22, 1853, Boston, Mass.
  d. June 20, 1920, San Francisco, Calif.
  U. S. Representative, 1893-99
MARKHAM, Henry H.
  b. Nov. 16, 1840, Essex County, N.Y.
  d. Oct. 9, 1823, Pasadena, Calif.
  U. S. Representative, 1885-87
  Governor, 1891-95
MARSHALL, Edward C.
  b. June 29, 1821, Woodford County, Ky.
  d. July 9, 1893, San Francisco, Calif.
  U. S. Representative, 1851-53
METCALF, Victor H.
  b. Oct. 10, 1853, Utica, N. Y.
  d. Feb. 30, 1936, Oakland, Calif.
  U. S. Representative, 1899-1904
  Secretary of Commerce and Labor, 1904-06
MILLER, John F.
  b. Nov. 21, 1831, South Bend, Ind.
  d. Mar. 8, 1886, Washington, D. C.
  U. S. Senator, 1881-86
MORROW, William W.
  b. July 15, 1843, Wayne County, Ind.
  d. July 24, 1929, San Francisco, Calif.
  U. S. Representative, 1885-91
NEEDHAM, James C.
  b. Sept. 17, 1864, Carson City, Nev.
  d. July 11, 1942, Modesto, Calif.
  U. S. Representative, 1899-1913
NIXON, Richard M.
  b. Jan. 9, 1913, Yorba Linda, Calif.
  U. S. Representative, 1947-49
  U. S. Senator, 1949-53
  U. S. Vice-President, 1953-61
  U. S. President, 1969-
NOLAN, John I.
  b. Jan. 14, 1874, San Francisco, Calif.
  d. Nov. 18, 1922, San Francisco, Calif.
  U. S. Representative, 1913-22

OLSON, Culbert L.
  b. Nov. 7, 1876, Fillmore, Utah
  d. Apr. 13, 1962, Los Angeles, Calif.
  Governor, 1939-43
OSBORNE, Henry Z.
  b. Oct. 4, 1848, New Lebanon, N.Y.
  d. Feb. 8, 1923, Los Angeles, Calif.
  U. S. Representative, 1917-23
PACHECO, Romualdo
  b. Oct. 31, 1831, Santa Barbara, Calif.
  d. Jan. 23, 1899, Oakland, Calif.
  Governor, 1875-77
  U. S. Representative, 1877-83
PAGE, Horace F.
  b. Oct. 20, 1833, Orleans County, N.Y.
  d. Aug. 23, 1890, San Francisco, Calif.
  U. S. Representative, 1873-83
PARDEE, George C.
  b. July 25, 1857, San Francisco, Calif.
  d. Sept. 1, 1947, Oakland, Calif.
  Governor, 1903-07
PERKINS, George C.
  b. Aug. 23, 1839, Kennebunkport, Me.
  d. Feb. 26, 1923, Oakland, Calif.
  Governor, 1879-83
  U. S. Senator, 1893-1915
PHELPS, Timothy G.
  b. Dec. 20, 1824, Chenango County, N.Y.
  d. June 11, 1899, San Carlos, Calif.
  U. S. Representative, 1861-63
PIPER, William A.
  b. May 21, 1826, Franklin County, Pa.
  d. Aug. 5, 1899, San Francisco, Calif.
  U. S. Representative, 1875-77
RAKER, John E.
  b. July 22, 1863, Knox County, Ill.
  d. Dec. 6, 1926, Washington, D. C.
  U. S. Representative, 1911-26
RANDALL, Charles H.
  b. July 23, 1865, Nemaha, Wisc.
  d. Feb. 18, 1951, Los Angeles, Calif.
  U. S. Representative, 1915-21

RILEY, Bennett
 b. Nov. 27, 1787, in New York
 d. June 9, 1853, Buffalo, N. Y.
 Provisional governor, 1849
ROLPH, Thomas
 b. Jan. 17, 1885, San Francisco, Calif.
 d. May 10, 1956, San Francisco, Calif.
 Governor, 1931-35
 U. S. Representative, 1941-45
ROSECRANS, William S.
 b. Sept. 6, 1819, Kingston, O.
 d. Mar. 11, 1898, Los Angeles, Calif.
 Union general, 1861-65
 U. S. Representative, 1881-85
SARGENT, Aaron A.
 b. Sept. 28, 1827, Newburyport, Mass.
 d. Aug. 14, 1887, San Francisco, Calif.
 U. S. Representative, 1861-63, 1869-73
 U. S. Senator, 1873-79
SCOTT, Charles L.
 b. Jan. 23, 1827, Richmond, Va.
 d. Apr. 30, 1899, Monroe County, La.
 U. S. Representative, 1857-61
SHANNON, Thomas B.
 b. Sept. 21, 1827, Westmoreland County, Pa.
 d. Feb. 21, 1897, San Francisco, Calif.
 U. S. Representative, 1863-65
SHORTRIDGE, Samuel M.
 b. Aug. 3, 1861, Mt. Pleasant, Ia.
 d. Jan. 15, 1952, Atherton, Calif.
 U. S. Senator, 1921-33
SMITH, Persifor F.
 b. Nov. 16, 1798, Philadelphia, Pa.
 d. May 17, 1858, Ft. Leavenworth, Kan.
 Provisional governor, 1849
SMITH, Sylvester C.
 b. Aug. 26, 1858, Mt. Pleasant, Ia.
 d. Jan. 26, 1913, Los Angeles, Calif.
 U. S. Representative, 1905-13
STANFORD, Leland
 b. Mar. 9, 1824, Warervliet, N. Y.
 d. June 21, 1893, Palo Alto, Calif.
 Governor, 1862-63
 U. S. Senator, 1885-93

STEPHENS, William D.
  b. Dec. 26, 1859, Easton, O.
  d. Apr. 25, 1944, Los Angeles, Calif.
  U. S. Representative, 1911-16
  Governor, 1917-23
STONEMAN, George
  b. Aug. 8, 1822, Busti, N.Y.
  d. Sept. 5, 1894, Buffalo, N.Y.
  Governor, 1883-87
STUBBS, Henry E.
  b. Mar. 4, 1881, Nampa, Tex.
  d. Feb. 28, 1937, Washington, D. C.
  U. S. Representative, 1933-37
SUMNER, Charles A.
  b. Aug. 2, 1835, Great Barrington, Mass.
  d. Jan. 31, 1903, San Francisco, Calif.
  U. S. Representative, 1883-85
THOMPSON, Thomas L.
  b. May 31, 1838, Charleston, W.Va.
  d. Feb. 1, 1898, Santa Rosa, Calif.
  U. S. Representative, 1887-89
TOLAN, John H.
  b. Jan. 15, 1877, St. Peter, Minn.
  d. June 30, 1947, Westwood, Calif.
  U. S. Representative, 1935-47
TRAEGER, William I.
  b. Feb. 26, 1880, Porterville, Calif.
  d. Jan. 20, 1935, Los Angeles, Calif.
  U. S. Representative, 1933-35
TULLY, Pleasant B.
  b. Mar. 21, 1829, Henderson County, Tex.
  d. Mar. 24, 1897, Gilroy, Calif.
  U. S. Representative, 1883-85
VANDEVER, William
  b. Mar. 21, 1817, Baltimore, Md.
  d. July 23, 1893, Ventura, Calif.
  U. S. Representative (Ia.), 1859-61
  U. S. Representative, 1887-91
WARREN, Earl
  b. Mar. 19, 1891, Los Angeles, Calif.
  Governor, 1943-53
  Chief Justice of U. S., 1953-69

WATERS, Russell
  b. June 6, 1843, Halifax, Vt.
  d. Sept. 25, 1911, Los Angeles, Calif.
  U. S. Representative, 1899-1901
WELCH, Richard J.
  b. Feb. 13, 1869, Monroe County, N.Y.
  d. Sept. 10, 1949, Needles, Calif.
  U. S.Representative, 1926-49
WELLER, John B.
  b. Feb. 22, 1812, Hamilton, O.
  d. Aug. 17, 1875, New Orleans, La.
  U. S. Senator, 1851-57
  Governor, 1858-60
  Minister to Mexico, 1860-61
WHITE, Stephen M.
  b. Jan. 19, 1853, San Francisco, Calif.
  d. Feb. 21, 1901, Los Angeles, Calif.
  U. S. Senator, 1893-99
WIGGINTON, Peter D.
  b. Sept. 6, 1839, Springfield, Ill.
  d. July 7, 1890, Oakland, Calif.
  U. S. Representative, 1875-79
WILLIAMS, Abram P.
  b. Feb. 3, 1832, New Portland, Me.
  d. Oct. 17, 1911, San Francisco, Calif.
  U. S. Senator, 1886-87
WOODS, Samuel D.
  b. Sept. 19, 1845, Mt. Pleasant, Tenn.
  d. Dec. 24, 1915, San Francisco, Calif.
  U. S. Representative, 1900-03
WORKS, John D.
  b. Mar. 29, 1847, Rising Sun, Ind.
  d. June 6, 1928, Los Angeles, Calif.
  U. S. Senator, 1911-15
WYNN, William J.
  b. June 12, 1860, San Francisco, Calif.
  d. Jan. 4, 1935, San Francisco, Calif.
  U. S. Representative, 1903-05
YOUNG, Clement C.
  b. Apr. 28, 1869, Lisbon, N.Y.
  d. Dec. 25, 1947, Berkeley, Calif.
  Governor, 1927-31

OUTLINE OF CONSTITUTION

I. Declaration of Rights
Sec. 1. Inalienable rights
Sec. 2. Purpose of government
Sec. 3. United States constitution
supreme law
Sec. 4. Liberty of conscience
Sec. 5. Suspension of habeas corpus
Sec. 6. Bail; unusual punishment;
detention of witnesses
Sec. 7. Trial by jury
Sec. 8. Pleading guilty before magistrate;
prosecutions; grand juries
Sec. 9. Liberty of speech and of the press
Sec. 10. Right to assemble and to petition
Sec. 11. Uniform general laws
Sec. 12. Civil power supreme; the military
Sec. 13. Criminal prosecutions; rights of
accused; due process of law;
jeopardy; comment on failure of
defendant to testify; depositions
Sec. 14. Eminent domain
Sec. 14½ Acquisition of land for public
improvements; excess condemnation
Sec. 15. No imprisonment for debt
Sec. 16. Bill of attainder; ex post facto
law; obligation of contract
Sec. 17. Rights of aliens
Sec. 18. Slavery prohibited
Sec. 19. Unreasonable seizure and search;
warrant
Sec. 20. Treason
Sec. 21. Privileges and immunities
Sec. 22. Constitution mandatory and pro-
hibitory
Sec. 23. Rights reserved
Sec. 24. No property qualification for
electors

V. Executive Department

VI. Judicial Department

XIV. Water and Water Rights

XV. Harbor Frontages

Sec. 1. Frontages on navigable waters may
be taken by eminent domain
Sec. 2. People shall always have access
to navigable waters
Sec. 3. Tidelands not to pass into
private hands

XVI. State Indebtedness

Sec. 1. State indebtedness; state
allocation board
Sec. 2. 1919 highway bonds
Sec. 3. Highway bonds; state highway
finance board
Sec. 4. State and university building
bonds
Sec. $4\frac{1}{2}$ State construction program bonds
(1955 Act)
Sec. 5. California olympiad bonds
Sec. 6. Veterans' farm and home bonds
(1949 Act)
Sec. 7. State park bonds
Sec. 8. San francisco harbor bonds
Sec. $8\frac{1}{2}$ Harbor development bonds; 1958
Sec. 9. Unemployment relief bonds
(1933 Act)
Sec. 10. Unemployment relief bonds; 1934
Sec. 11. Administration of relief
Sec. 12. Release of encumbrances given as
security for aid to aged
Sec. 13. Releasing all rights and encum-
brances taken as security for aid
to aged
Sec. 14. [None adopted]
Sec. 15. School bonds
Sec. 16. Veterans farm and home bonds
Sec.16.5. School bonds; 1952
Sec. 17. School bonds; 1954

DOCUMENTS

The history of California is so rich in detail, and has been so exhaustively treated by so many writers, that it is difficult to select documents which are representative but have not already been published in numerous other sources. The three which appear in this volume are chosen primarily for the contemporary viewpoint they embody -- a viewpoint not always accepted by later ages.

In the *Annals of the American Academy* in 1898, Professor R. D. Hunt published an article on "The Legal Status of California, 1846-49," when a confusing intermixture of local adventurism and quasi-official military intervention was hastening the end of the tottering Mexican regime. Following this is an impassioned editorial comment on the speech of William H. Seward of New York, in which Seward justified the admission of California to the Union as a free state to the considerable distaste of the writer in the *Southern Literary Messenger*, a widely-read journal of the mid-nineteenth century.

Most glamorous of all, however, are contemporary views of the Gold Rush of 1849 and the years following, and the concluding selection is an eyewitness account of San Francisco and the mining camps, published in New York by the Forty-Niner, C. H. Haskins, under the title *Argonauts of California.*

LEGAL STATUS OF CALIFORNIA, 1846-49

by R. D. Hunt

The United States in its federal capacity is required to guarantee to every state in the union a republican form of government. This implies the establishment of some government within each state, and hence a constitutional convention. New states to be formed out of territory of the United States, organized under its authority or acquired in an organized condition from foreign states, call for a second class of conventions to frame constitutions for such states. Such conventions are regularly assembled in pursuance of enabling acts of Congress. But there is another limited variety of conventions including such as have been convened by the inhabitants, or the temporary governments of organized territories, irregularly, without enabling acts of Congress. Among this last, or irregular class, Dr. Jameson mentions, somewhat inaccurately, the California convention of 1849.* Certainly the California convention was irregular; but it is well known that previous to the convention, California was not an organized territory of the United States; also that the convention did not meet at the free instance of the inhabitants. Not only so, but it will also plainly appear as the discussion proceeds, that the conditions under which the first California convention was held were wholly without exact precedent.†

The actual conquest of California by Americans was signalized by the hoisting of the Bear Flag at Sonoma, on June 15, 1846, by a few men under command of Captain Frémont. This rude but long since famous flag bore under the emblems of the lone star and grizzly bear the legend, "California Republic." Whatever may have been Frémont's real motives in this apparently almost wanton revolt, it is certain that his followers had little or no intention of erecting

* Jameson, "The Constitutional Convention," p. 178.
† See Gwin's exposition, Browne's "Debates," p. 393.

a permanent republic on the Pacific coast, but that for the most part they were patriotic Americans. The anomaly known as the California Republic was, as an independent government, insignificant, and extremely short-lived.

On July 7, Commodore Sloat, who had arrived a few days earlier, formally took possession of Monterey, the early capital of California. As soon as the Stars and Stripes floated over the land, the Bear Flag party abandoned the purpose of an independent revolution and the Bear Flag itself was superseded by our national ensign. Commodore Stockton arrived July 15, and succeeded Sloat at the desire and request of the latter, as commander-in-chief of all forces and operations on land, assuming active command shortly after his arrival. Sloat had lacked sympathy with the American revolutionists, and his conservative policy forbade his utilizing the forces of Frémont; but Stockton, having learned of the state of war while in Mexico, immediately adopted an aggressive policy, and decided to extend the occupation to the south territory. He accordingly organized the forces of Frémont as the California Battalion of Mounted Riflemen, which proved instrumental in completing the conquest.* Thus, then, while war was in progress between the United States and Mexico, the Mexican province of California was taken military possession of by United States forces.

On assuming command, Commodore Stockton had issued an undignified and impolitic address to the people, which in its tone was an offensive declaration of martial law.† This address neither embodied the views of Commodore Sloat nor conformed with the governmental policy at Washington.‡

* The conquest was easily accomplished, without a single important battle. Bidwell in *Century*, Vol. xli, p. 523.

† House Executive Documents, First Session, Thirty-first Congress, Vol. i, pp. 31–33.

‡ As witness its closing sentence : "As soon, therefore, as the officers of the civil law return to their respective duties, under a regularly organized government, and give security to life, liberty, and prosperity alike to all, the forces will be withdrawn, and the people left to manage their own affairs in their own way."

It was the fixed purpose of the administration at Washington to retain this country and make of it a permanent part of our national territory. Stockton, it would appear from his address, did not care to make California a territory of the United States; nor did he appear to desire any of its lands for his government.* His address scarcely contained a hint that it was to be held until a treaty should be concluded between the United States and Mexico. His alleged motive for completing the conquest was "to bestow peace and good order on the country:" this, however, was obviously inadequate and secondary.

California was now conquered territory. As such it could have no determinate status on a peace basis while war with Mexico continued; nor was it yet a part of the United States territory, except as a temporary military possession. The Department of California was conquered territory subject to temporary military control. Now conquered territory, according to a well-defined principle of international law, regularly retains its prior municipal institutions, the conqueror being authorized to ordain needful temporary laws and regulations.† The laws of Mexico which had hitherto obtained in California should have been continued by the military rulers of the country until those rulers had put in operation some other provisional government;‡ and indeed this principle was distinctly proclaimed by Commodore

---

* Bancroft, " History of California," Vol. v, p. 258.

† This is the view, in the main, that I conceive President Polk, not with strict consistency, to have held. See his Message to Congress, December 8, 1846. But in Congress widely divergent views were adhered to. Mr. Douglas held that the province belonged to the United States by conquest, and that no proclamation was needed to make it ours. Mr. Rhett, at the other extreme, urged that the conquered territory rested on the power of the sword alone, whether the government was civil or military in character. Mr. Bayly declared the President to be a usurper in establishing or authorizing civil government in the conquered territory. Mr. Seddon approximated the President's position, holding it to be the right and duty of the military commanders to establish provisional civil government, and maintaining the power of annexation and incorporation to be the prerogative of the conquering nation, to be exercised, however, only by Congress.— *Congressional Globe*, 1846-47, pp. 14, 15, 23-26, 75.

‡ *California Star*, June 19, 1847.

Stockton who, on August 17, 1846, issued from Los Angeles a proclamation to the people in which he said, in part:

"The Territory of California now belongs to the United States, and will be governed as soon as circumstances may permit, by officers and laws similar to those by which the other territories of the United States are regulated and protected. But until the Governor, the Secretary, and council are appointed, and the various civil departments of the government are arranged, military laws will prevail, and the Commander-in-Chief will be the Governor and protector of the territory. In the meantime the people will be permitted, and are now requested to meet in their several towns and departments, at such time and place as they may see fit to elect civil officers and fill the places of those who decline to continue in office; and to administer the laws according to the former usages of the territory. In all cases where people fail to elect, the Commander-in-Chief will make the appointments himself." *

This proclamation put in force at the same time two kinds of law, the one civil, the other military. Many deemed them irreconcilable: but the temporary existence of military rule is plainly not inconsistent with the perpetuation of the civil institutions and regular administration of justice of the conquered province. The military commander is clothed with certain civil functions; the civil laws and their officers receive their sanction from the military domination.† But while the civil law of Mexico was thus proclaimed, and the President assumed that a temporary government was in operation, as a matter of fact Mexican law never was, and from the nature of the case could not be, put in full operation

* *California Star*, January 9, 1847.

† The *Star*, January 16, 1847, gave a lucid exposition of the reconciliation of laws. It said, in part : " Military law does not affect the citizens in their private relations with each other . . . . it affects them only in their relations to their government. . . . . The courts of the country are never brought under the influence of martial law, but are only affected by it in their character of private individuals and not as courts; and unless their proceedings are entirely superseded, they must be governed by the civil or municipal laws alone." The question of the co-existence of civil government and military rule was being discussed almost simultaneously in Congress. Mr. Douglas had said: " Without some form of civil government, all must be anarchy, and riot." Mr. Seddon had ably argued the continuance of the civil institutions and regular administration of justice of the conquered province. —*Congressional Globe*, 1846–47, pp. 15, 24.

after the American conquest, and the military commander
had not established any satisfactory civil government in its
stead.* Almost immediately after the conquest, the American inhabitants began to complain, not only of the
inadequacy and want of uniformity in the Mexican laws
theoretically in force, but also of the actual absence of any
rational system of law. This just complaint was destined to
grow louder and more bitter from the moment of the conquest till the eve of the Constitutional Convention.

There was much uncertainty as to what laws were in force
at a given moment. As early as January 9, 1847, the
California Star reflects the not uncommon feeling of dissat-
isfied uncertainty. The alcalde was the sole judicial officer
of California at this period. Among native Californians the
functions of the alcalde had been perpetuated by tradition.
One such officer retained jurisdiction at each centre of
population. This jurisdiction had come to be exceedingly
vague, variable, and uncertain in scope. The much-
talked-of Mexican system of law, theoretically continued
in full operation, was in reality narrowed down to a
number of local alcaldes, the most powerful one being
resident at Monterey, but each having an indeterminate
status. Inadequate as was this system of district judges
under later Mexican rule, it was vastly more unsatisfactory
as well as positively distasteful to progressive Americans:
"hard headed American pioneers demanded a better system
of government than the Mexican law gave them." †

Since Americans began to succeed Mexicans, or Spaniards,
as alcaldes, almost immediately following the conquest, the
growth of American law was inevitably rapid. While theoretically the Mexican civil law continued in force, in fact

---

* *California Star*, June 19, 1847, also *Alta California*, June 14, 1849, and earlier
dates.

† Fitch, in the *Century*, Vol. **xl**, p. 779. On the alcalde, see Royce, "California,"
pp. 200 et seq.; Hittell, "History of California," Vol. ii, pp. 656 et seq.; Moses,
"Municipal Government in San Francisco," pp. 95 et seq.; newspapers of the
period, etc.

the Americans, more especially the newly appointed alcaldes, had brought their own notions of common law principles and forms. At once a process of amalgamation was commenced, and very naturally the American law—not very accurately represented, to be sure—rapidly supplanted the obsolescent customs and procedure. Although there seems to have been no early official decree to warrant it, the trial by jury * was soon in common practice, fairly well defined and understood, and sanctioned by the governor.† Likewise it was recognized that the English language would inevitably supplant the Spanish.‡

Commodore Stockton had prepared a plan for civil government, and had drafted a constitution; but this was never put in full operation. His purpose was thwarted by a serious revolt of the natives, to put down which involved considerable time and fighting and some bloodshed. Before the authorities were again in a position to undertake better civil organization, their plans were interfered with by several important and unexpected events. General Kearny entered California in November, 1846, and shortly afterward followed the unfortunate controversy as to the relative positions of the two officers.§

Who possessed the rightful authority to govern the conquered territory? The actual status of the country at the time of Kearny's arrival had not been, and could not be anticipated by Kearny's instructions. Weakened and humbled at San Pascual, his consciously delicate situation doubtless had much influence in deciding him to refrain

---

* Nothing like the trial by jury was known to the Mexican system ; but Walter Colton, the first American alcalde of Monterey, summoned at the early date of September 4, 1846, the first jury in California, he having been in office scarcely a month. Hittell, *op. cit.* Vol. ii, p. 663 ; Bancroft, *op. cit.* Vol. vi, p. 258.

† Mason's general order, issued December 29, 1847, directed trials by jury in all cases before the alcaldes' courts where the amount involved exceeded one hundred dollars. House Executive Documents, First Session, Thirty-first Congress, Vol. xvii, p. 452 ; Hittell, *op. cit.* Vol. ii, p. 664.

‡ *Californian,* October 10, 1846.

§ For details and evidence on both sides of this controversy, consult Bancroft, *op. cit.* Vol. vi, Cap. xvi, especially foot-notes.

from asserting his claim to the chief command at that time. Stockton even states that he proffered Kearny the chief command, and that the latter declined it. Even assuming as established that Kearny originally had the right to command, it is easy to understand how, under the peculiar circumstances, Stockton might come to regard himself as possessing permanent precedence. So, when a little later Kearny asserted his authority, Stockton firmly refused to recognize it. The controversy deepened; Kearny, having an insufficient command to enforce his claims, decided to await further instructions from Washington; it is certain that Stockton was generally recognized by the people as military commander and territorial governor until the date of his departure. On January 14, 1847, he tendered Colonel Frémont his commission as governor of the territory. For a term of perhaps fifty days Frémont, having acted in direct disobedience to Kearny's orders, was quite generally recognized as governor; during these days Kearny's claims were of course not relinquished. Instructions came in February positively directing that the senior officer of the land forces (Kearny) should be civil governor. Then followed the Frémont-Kearny controversy the upshot of which was the court-martial of Frémont, his conviction, and subsequent remission of punishment.

On March 1 General Kearny, jointly with Commodore Shubrick, then commander of the naval forces as Stockton's successor, issued a circular in which he formally assumed the governorship, and designated Monterey as the capital.* This proclamation seems to have had the immediate effect

* " California Message and Correspondence," pp. 288-89. I quote a portion to show the status as he conceived it, and the good intentions looking to an organized government: " The President of the United States having instructed the undersigned to take charge of the civil government of California, he enters upon his duties with an ardent desire to promote, as far as he is able, the interests of the country and the welfare of its inhabitants. . . It is the wish and design of the United States to provide for California with the least possible delay, a free government similar to those in her other territories; and the people will soon be called upon to exercise their rights as freemen, in electing their own representatives to make such laws as may be deemed best for their interests and welfare."

of encouraging the Americans to look for the peace and
tranquillity which should follow upon the establishment of
the civil government expected.*   But the civil government,
now so long anticipated, was not yet forthcoming; affairs
continued in their extremely uncertain and almost chaotic
state.   Honest seekers after laws were unable to find them:
the desideratum of exact statutes was unattainable to those
common-sense pioneers.   An interesting editorial, on " The
Laws in Force," in the *Star* of March 27 says, in part:

" Some contend that there are really no laws in force here, but the
divine law and the law of nature, while others are of the opinion that
there *are* laws in force here if they could only be found. . . Both
sides, however, seem to agree that the ' former usages ' have been in
force. . . We have not been able to discover any traces of written
law particularly applicable to this territory except the Bandos of the
Alcaldes which could not have been intended to apply to any except
those within their jurisdiction. We have frequently heard it stated
that there are general written laws of the people of the whole territory, but we have not as yet been able to discover their ' whereabouts.'
. . . It seems to us that the continuance of the former laws in
force, when it is impossible to produce them in any court in the
country, or for the people to ascertain what they are, will be produc-
tive of confusion and difficulty."

Civil government to the non-Spanish reading Americans
in California at this period was obviously entirely wanting
as an objective reality.   The growing dissatisfaction did not
pass unexpressed; ominous murmurings began to be heard,
and the alleged right of self-government found frequent
utterance.†

* See editorial in *Californian*, March 13, 1847.

† As early as August, 1846, the claim of the right of self-government began to be
asserted. In the first number of the *Californian* is an editorial on the " Prospects
of California," in which the editors affirm : " No impediment now exists to the
establishment of a colonial government in California, all patriotic citizens should
unite at once for this purpose." In the *Star* (April 17, 1847) a correspondent
declares: " The people themselves, independently of Mexico, and with the consent
of the officers of the United States now in command, have perfect right to enact
laws for their own government."

While the early American settlers were dilating upon their wrongs and clamor-
ing for their supposed rights, it scarcely occurred to them that on technical
grounds it might be urged that they themselves were aliens to the United

On May 31, 1847, General Kearny left Monterey on his
return to the United States, being succeeded in military and
civil command by Colonel R. B. Mason, who was thus
military commander with full power to establish temporary
civil government.   A single sentence from Secretary Marcy's
letter of instructions will serve to indicate his position as
contemplated by the administration:

"Under the law of nations the power conquering a territory or
country has a right to establish a civil government within the same,
as a means of securing the conquest, and with a view to protecting
the persons and property of the people, and it is not intended to
limit you in the full exercise of this authority."*

Pending the establishment of a temporary civil government, the territory was plainly under military rule, and it is
an unmistakable inference from his correspondence that
Mason considered the supreme power vested in himself as
senior military officer.† He heard the clamors for better
organization, he recognized the needs of the American
settlers as well as the disaffection of the Californians; but he
felt the strictures of his own belligerent authority, and
assumed, perhaps wisely, a conservative attitude.   He expected within a very short time to " have the good tidings
of peace," which should bring the certainty that California
would forever belong to the United States.‡ While proclaim-
ing the continued existence of former institutions and usages,
as his predecessor had done, he virtually acknowledged his
ignorance of the most important of these institutions:§ and

States in conquered territory. So far from considering themselves a *conquered*
people, they took to themselves, in large measure, the credit of being the real
conquerors, —for had they not welcomed the American forces, and rendered their
commanders invaluable assistance ?   While they had left the United States, they
yet accounted themselves perfectly loyal Americans, and rationally viewed, they
were right.   The highly strained and technical view that they were military
captives (See Royce, "California," p. 200) hardly merits more than a mere mention.   Manifest destiny had decreed California to become a part of our union.

  *"California Message and Correspondence," pp. 244-45.
  † Ibid., pp. 317-18, 321.
  ‡ Ibid., pp. 318-19.
  § Ibid., pp. 317, 322; *California Star*, April 8, 1848, correspondence of "Pacific."

so that *quasi*-patriarchal officer, known as alcalde, was continued in the exercise of increasingly elastic and indefinite powers.

But notwithstanding the fact that Colonel Mason faithfully studied the situation, it became more and more evident that while the war with Mexico should continue, no satisfactory organization on the old Mexican basis could be reached. No action in Congress was now longer reasonably to be expected; Mason, as military ruler, maintained a strictly conservative policy and hoped for tidings of peace.* Meanwhile, he set about discovering and formulating the "principal features of Mexican law applicable to the country at the time of the conquest." A few days before the news of peace reached him, he had ready for publication a code of laws "for the better government of California." This code, a volume of 140 pages, is said to have been printed in the English and Spanish languages; but on receipt of tidings of peace, Governor Mason withheld its publication, and so the much talked of, but ever invisible, "former laws and usages," of Mexico, theoretically in force in California, were destined to remain undiscovered to the eager Americans, nor was any attempt ever made to enforce the laws thus codified and thus withheld from the people.†

The territory of California was, then, under strict military rule during that period of Colonel Mason's governorship ending with the tidings of peace with Mexico, received August 6, 1848. Under the military rule the American settlers grew exceedingly restive; their murmuring became ominous growling and bitter complaint. The newspapers of the day reflect the general discontent.‡ The very absence of fixed, well-defined and generally understood law evoked

---

* The *Californian*, May 3, 1847, says editorially: "We have been credibly informed that Governor Mason has relinquished the project of a civil organization . . . . as he is in daily expectation of a communication from Washington probably appointing a governor and furnishing a pattern-code of laws."

† *Californian*, August 14, 1848; *Alta California*, June 4, 1849.

‡ See the *California Star*, June 26, *Californian*, June 5, 12, etc.

the loudest complaints.   As the months passed, as immigration increased, as the country became gradually developed— all without a uniform system of law and with a government which no one understood,—the Americans conceived their already grievous wrongs greatly aggravated; hence the situation, already long unsatisfactory, was fast becoming critical.*   The more radical of the settlers began vigorously to denounce the early officers of the conquest and violently to assail the military government, and under the highly disturbed and half-chaotic condition of affairs there was incitement toward the movement of popular self-government.†

The discovery of gold early in 1848 was an event not calculated to mitigate the gravity of the situation. Some sort of law was made absolutely imperative by the great influx of gold hunters from all nations. The discovery gave an enormous impetus to the movement toward popular organization, especially state organization, and proved to Congress the futility of dallying longer with the question.

We have now followed the main current of political events in the province of California from the American conquest to the ratification of the treaty of peace between the United States and Mexico. The California Republic, proclaimed by Frémont, was nominal, short-lived, and, as a separate government, insignificant. The succeeding governors from Sloat to Mason held office by virtue of military, or naval rank. While the administrations of these rulers varied in efficiency, while their instructions usually allowed wide discretionary powers and were not always consistent, and while local conditions were constantly and materially changing, there was always military domination, under forms varying from merely nominal authority to strict martial law, up to the moment the treaty was ratified.

* See the contemporaneous journals, especially " Pacific's " correspondence in the *Star*, April 8, 1848, and *Californian*, February 2, 1848.

† See controversy between " Pacific" and "Sober Second Thought " in the *Californian*, January-February, 1848.

Under this dominion, and deriving its sanction from it, was the effete, unsuited and increasingly unsatisfactory civil government, previously existent in the province, and now imperfectly perpetuated. Although the later military governors especially were given full power to establish a suitable temporary government, no such government was ever put in operation.

The Treaty of Guadalupe Hidalgo was concluded on February 2, 1848, and duly ratified at Querétaro on May 30. By its terms the territory of California was ceded to the United States, of which it became completely a part. News of the treaty reached California on August 6, and it was announced on the following day in a proclamation by Governor Mason. Of course there could be no apparent change in the government of the territory until after August 6; but technically from the moment of the ratification of the treaty the military rule was ended, and hence ceased to have obligatory authority. California now entered her most critical period, so often and so justly characterized as the "No-Government Period."* In his proclamation announcing the treaty Mason takes an extremely hopeful view of the situation, and believes that "instead of revolutions and insurrections there will be internal tranquillity; instead of a fickle and vacillating policy, there will be a firm and stable government, administering justice with impartiality, and punishing crime with the strong arm of power."† He is fully convinced that Congress will soon confer upon the people the "constitutional rights of citizens of the United States," that a regular territorial government will be an accomplished fact, and

" There is every reason to believe that Congress has already passed the act, and that a civil government is now on its way to this country,

* Bayard Taylor, "Eldorado" p. 146. Mr. Fitch asserts: "There was absolutely no precedent for the cession of the territory, and the neglect of Congress to provide territorial officers left California in the unique position of a land without a government."—*Century*, Vol. xl, p. 782; see Semple's statement in Convention, Browne's "Debates," p. 23.

† In the *Californian*, September 2, 1848.

to replace that which has been organized under the rights of conquest."

Unfortunately the civil government was not so near at hand. California was destined to continue through many trying months practically without any organized form of government.

The great migrations to the land of gold had begun, for California had become the "focus of the world's attention," and was "to be morally and socially tried as no other American community ever has been tried."* Mason continued as *de facto* head of the *quasi*-civil government under military rule, in daily expectation of instructions from Washington. He admitted that the territory was without civil government, and yet, keenly awake to the conditions as they then existed, he suffered technicalities to give way to practical common sense, judicially applied.†

The first session of the Thirtieth Congress adjourned August 14, leaving California in an anomalous condition. This fact was fully recognized by the President, who announced, through Secretary Buchanan, the existence of a *de facto* government, justifying it by the "great law of necessity."‡ "The termination of the war," wrote the secretary, "left an existing government *de facto*, in full operation, and this will continue, with the presumed consent of the people, until Congress shall provide for them a territorial government." In November, before it was known that Congress had adjourned without providing for its government, Commodore Jones arrived and held a conference with Acting-Governor Mason. Both were impressed with the necessity of immediate action, and they agreed that in default of the arrival of the sloop *St. Mary's* with the long-expected territorial government, the people should be encouraged to appoint delegates who should "frame laws and

* Royce, "California," pp. 221-22, see Hittell, *op. cit.*, Vol. ii, p. 675.
† "California Message and Correspondence," p. 497.
‡ See Buchanan's letter, "California Message and Correspondence," pp. 6-9: it bears the date of October 9, 1848.

make other necessary arrangements for a provisional government of California."*

The arrival of the *St. Mary's* with the not altogether unanticipated news of congressional failure to provide settled the question of territorial government during 1848. Secretary Buchanan, in his open letter to the people, advised them to "live peaceably and quietly under the existing government;" but to those conversant with the character of that *de facto* government and the rapidly shifting conditions—and to none more certainly than to Colonel Mason—it was perfectly obvious that to comply with Buchanan's request was daily becoming more difficult, and fast approaching the impossible. Even before the letter arrived, the people had begun to act upon their convictions. The "uncertain, amphibious character"† of the ruler and his strict adherence to a conservative policy, the vast influx of an extremely heterogeneous population, the daily augmentation of the criminal class and increase of depredations upon life and property, and the impotence of the half-Mexican, half-American judicial system are among the causes which appealed to all good citizens to be active in the organization of some suitable government with the least possible delay.

The first preparatory movement of the kind was an enthusiastic meeting of the citizens of Pueblo de San José.‡ Provisional government meetings, after the first of December, were frequent in San Francisco, San José and other leading towns of the territory. The sentiment in favor of a popular provisional government seems to have been practically unanimous among the thinking people. Stirring resolutions, drafted by some of the best legal talent of California, were adopted. The San José meeting recommended that a convention "for the purpose of nominating a suitable candidate for governor," and other suitable business, be held at that

---

* *Star and Californian*, November 25, 1848.
† Von Holst, "History of the United States," Vol. iii, p. 462.
‡ December 11, 1848. See *Star and Californian*, December 16.

place on the second Monday in January, 1849.* At San
Francisco a similar recommendation was adopted, the date
of the proposed convention being fixed at the first Monday
in March, 1849.† On February 12 the people of San Francisco met in mass meeting and established a temporary government for that district.‡ Thus the legislative assembly
of San Francisco, comprising among its fifteen members the
ablest local representatives of the settlers' theory of the
legal status of California came into existence, with motives
whose patriotism cannot be impeached and members most
honored in California's annals.

On April 12, the *Iowa* landed with General Bennett Riley
on board, who, on the following day, relieved Colonel Mason
as Acting-Governor of California. On assuming command of
the civil affairs it was General Riley's intention to complete the
organization of the existing government and to call a convention "for forming a state constitution, or plan of territorial
government, to be submitted to Congress for its approval."§
But, on further consultation, he deemed it best to postpone
all such action until it might be ascertained what Congress had
done in the short session. The steamer *Edith* bore him the
information that the national legislature had again adjourned
without making any provision for the civil government of
California. He forthwith issued a proclamation, June 3,

"defining what was understood to be the legal position of affairs here,
and pointing out the course it was deemed advisable to pursue in order
to procure a new political organization better adapted to the character and present condition of the country."‖

* *Star and Californian*, December 23, 1848.
† Reasons for this proposed delay are set forth in the *Alta California*, January
4, 1849. Several dates were recommended by the various district meetings; but
finally the first Monday of August—a date remote enough to allow the southern
districts to be represented—was agreed upon. See *Alta California*, March 22.

‡ See address of the Assembly in reply to General Riley's proclamation against
that body; published in the *Alta California*, August 9, 1848. The address is
signed by Peter H. Burnett, Henry Harrison and S. R. Gerry.

§ See his letter to General Jones, "California Message and Correspondence,"
pp. 748-52.

‖ Ibid., p. 748. The proclamation is on pp 776-80; also in *Alta California*, June 14.

In this proclamation—which had doubtless been in contemplation for some time, and which showed a careful study of the situation—Governor Riley appointed the first day of August for the selection of delegates to a general convention, which should convene in Monterey on the first of September following, and proceed to form a state constitution or a plan for territorial government.

In the meantime General Riley had been made aware of the existence and force of the San Francisco Legislative Assembly, which in the absence of government (as it claimed) had been assuming new and extended powers. It did not recognize any *civil* power as residing in General Riley, a military officer, but deemed itself entitled to frame a temporary government for the protection of life and property in the district,* and to co-operate with the other districts in the movement toward popular organization. At this period, as throughout its short but useful career, the assembly was a loyal American body, numbering among its members many of California's most patriotic pioneers.† Considerable excitement was produced by the information that Congress had the second time failed to provide; this was greatly aggravated by the news of the extension of the revenue laws over California and the appointment of James Collier as collector. A public meeting being straightway held, a committee, with Peter Burnett as chairman, prepared an address protesting against the injustice of taxation without representation.‡ The assembly, through the committee's address, again took occasion to assert what it considered its undoubted right:

" It is the duty of the government of the United States to give us.

* See Lippitt's article in the *Century*, Vol. xl, especially p. 795.

† The *Alta California* makes a strong case in its justification of the existence and legislation of the assembly. See, for instance, an editorial, June 14, 1849.

‡ In *Alta California*, June 14, 1849. It says, in part: " For the first time in the history of the 'model Republic.' . . . the Congresses of the United States . . . have assumed the right not only to '*tax us without representation*,' *but to tax us without giving us any government at all*.' "

laws; and when that duty is not performed, one of the clearest rights we have left, is to govern ourselves."

Acting upon this supposed right, the assembly recommended a general convention to be held at San José on the third Monday in August,

"with enlarged discretion to deliberate upon the best measures to be taken; and to form, if they upon mature consideration should deem it advisable, a state constitution to be submitted to the people."

Before the address had been published, Governor Riley, fully cognizant of the powers assumed by the legislative assembly and of its recent actions, issued a proclamation* to the people of San Francisco, pronouncing the "body of men styling themselves the 'legislative assembly of the district of San Francisco'" an illegal and unauthorized body, which had usurped powers vested solely in the Congress of the United States, and warning all persons "not to countenance said illegal and unauthorized body, either by paying taxes or by supporting or abetting their officers."† Now the committee's address, which had been adopted before the promulgation of Riley's proclamation to the people of the district, was not published until a few days after the promulgation of the same. Thus there was an appearance of reckless defiance on the part of the assembly, which did not in fact exist.‡

But now, at last, in the middle of June, 1849, the opposing theories with reference to the legal status of California from the ratification of the treaty with Mexico to the adoption of the constitution on November 13, 1849, had been clearly defined and respectively defended in the territory itself. The two conflicting theories may be designated as the Settlers' Theory, sometimes called the Benton Theory; and the Administration Theory, sometimes called the

---

* "California Message and Correspondence," pp. 773-74.
† See Moses, *op. cit.*, p. 114; Bancroft, *op. cit.*, Vol. vi, pp. 277-78.
‡ See Burnett, "Recollections and Opinions of an Old Pioneer," pp. 325-26.

Buchanan Theory.* Since many of the salient features of
both these have necessarily been set forth in the narrative,
I must content myself with a rapid résumé, at this point.†
The leading advocate of the Settlers' Theory at Washington was Senator Benton. His recommendations to the
people were substantially what the citizens were at that
moment beginning of themselves to act upon in earnest.‡
Among the settlers themselves who were patriotic Americans
interested in the permanent welfare of California, there was
virtual unanimity of sentiment in favor of the Settlers'
Theory.§ Without doubt a large part of the discussion was
extremely passionate and biased; but that the moral and
political wrongs endured by California during these critical
months, and even years, were without parallel or precedent
in our Union, is perfectly patent to any one at all acquainted
with the conditions. One cannot expect an entirely dispas-
sionate discussion or a calmly judicial poise amid such
stirring, shifting, practical scenes in a place of world-con-
fluence and a time so justly characterized as the No-Government Period.

Stripping the argument of all passion, the Settlers'
Theory may be briefly stated as follows:|| The moment the
treaty of Guadalupe Hidalgo took effect, the Constitution

* These names are applied mainly on the ground of mere convenience. There
seems to be some doubt as to the exact position held by Buchanan and President
Polk during the latter part of this period. Governor Burnett was of opinion that
they adopted the view maintained by the more prominent settlers.—*Op. cit.*, p. 331.

† One of the best statements of the two theories extant is that of Burnett, *op.
cit.*, pp. 329 et seq. Royce has a good statement in his " California" pp. 247 et seq.
On this question see Mr. Botts' long speech in Browne's " Debates," pp. 274–84,
and consequent discussion.

‡ His letter is in *Alta California*, January 11, 1849; see editorial comments,
January 18.

§ See Burnett, *op. cit.*, p. 331, where he says: "Among the lawyers of California
who had been here long enough to understand the true merits of the controversy,
there was almost an entire unanimity in the opinion that only a *de facto* government could exist in the country, based upon the consent of the people. This was
the view of three-fourths of the inhabitants."

|| Allowance must of course be made in any construction of this theory as I have
here formulated it, for individual variation and hence slight latitude for deviation
in details.

of the United States and American principles were extended over the acquired territory of California. Although no territorial system of American civil law has been regularly extended over or established in California, the Mexican civil law has been in fact superseded. Congress, whose primary power to legislate is admitted,* failing to provide a territorial government, it is no usurpation in the people to legislate temporarily for themselves in self-defence. As matter of fact, the government established during the war, was, at its conclusion continued as *de facto* government; but whereas it had before derived its authority from the rights of war, it now has no such source of power, but derives its authority from the " presumed consent of the people." A subordinate military officer can no longer legally fill the office of governor except by the sufferance of the people. While their presumed consent was " irresistibly inferred " by Secretary Buchanan in an *a priori* manner, it was historically entirely unreal; instead of consent there was express dissent and repeated protest against the *de facto* government.† Again, since the President, through his secretary," urgently advises the people of California to live peaceably and quietly under the existing government," he evidently believes that the people had the *right* to change it. Because of the extraordinary exigencies of the situation, the Legislative Assembly of San Francisco was rightfully and legally formed, and the communities of Sonoma and Sacramento city followed the example, thus exercising temporary legislative power as the practical application of the rights implied by American citizenship.‡

Opposed to the Settlers' Theory was that which I have called the Administration Theory, which was maintained by

---

* This congresssional authority, however, was not universally admitted. Mr. Botts emphatically denied it. See his conclusions in Browne's " Debates," p. 284.

† See *Alta California.* August 9, 1849, and earlier dates; also Fitch, in the *Century,* Vol. xl, p. 783, etc.

‡ Report of governmental agent, Thomas B. King, as published in Frost's " History of the State of California," pp. 108 et seq.; also Fitch, *op cit.*

the last territorial governors, notably by General Riley. Riley
states his position, which is in accord with his instructions,
in his proclamation to the people given May 3, 1849. This
theory may be briefly summarized: Under a general principle of the law of nations, the laws of California, which were
proclaimed to be in force after the American conquest, must,
at the conclusion of peace with Mexico, continue in full
force until changed by competent authority. That authority
is vested solely in Congress. Hence, Congress failing to
make other provision for the territory, the system of laws,
defective as it is, which obtained under military rule, must
in so far as they are not inconsistent with the laws, constitutions, and treaties of the United States, continue in force
under the civil government *de facto ;* the commanding military officer, by virtue of a vacancy in the office of governor,
is *ex officio* civil governor. The Legislative Assembly of
San Francisco, or any similar body, therefore, purporting
to represent the people and presuming to legislate for them,
is an illegal and unauthorized body, having usurped powers
vested solely in the United States Congress.

I shall not attempt finally to decide this vexed question,
by a technical argument, in favor of the one theory or the
other. Without doubt, judged from a moral standpoint,
the settlers were in the right, and would on the social ground
of self-defence, have been justified in forming for themselves
a temporary territorial government. Fortunately for state
organization, as the event proved, they did not. On strictly
legal grounds, Riley's position was in the main probably
the more nearly correct, although he, as *ex officio* governor,
as well as the administration at Washington, failed to maintain complete consistency.

Shortly after General Riley's proclamation of May 3, in
which he appointed August 1, as the date for the election
of delegates who should meet in constitutional convention
in Monterey, on the first of September, events took place
which should serve at once to show the patriotism of the

leading settlers and to give additional color to the legality
of Riley's position.   What the people wanted was an organized government; the end was paramount, the means
secondary.   Hence indications of satisfaction with, and
acquiescence in Riley's plans began almost immediately to
manifest themselves.   The people of San José expressed
their satisfaction June 7, other districts followed them.   The
controverted points seem to have been waived by many, and
popular interest in the question of legal status was fast
waning.   On June 12 a committee of five from the San
Francisco Legislative Assembly had been appointed to cor-
respond with other districts relative to the proposed general convention of the people on their own authority.   The
committee, representing the stronghold of the Settlers'
Theory, viewing the changing situation and recognizing the
importance of success in the one desire of all parties, recommended the propriety "of acceding to the time and place
mentioned by General Riley, in his proclamation, and
acceded to by the people of some other districts."   This
concession, the committee held, was not one of principle,
but a matter of mere expediency, for they still refused to
recognize any rightful authority to *appoint* times and places
as residing in General Riley.*

Thus the controversy was practically at an end, and with
it died the mild revolution by the fiat of the people who
created it.   The legislative assembly ceased to exist.   The
members " were unwilling to use the powers vested by the
people in them for the production or perpetuation of civil
strife."†   The general acquiescence in the plans of General
Riley marked the emergence of California from a period of
most remarkable internal disquietude, characterized, however, by extremely little violence, and left little doubt of
speedy and satisfactory organization.‡

* *Alta California*, June 20, 1849 ; see Burnett, *op. cit.*, pp. 325-26.
† From the *Alta's* editorial on " The End of Revolution."
‡ In the early spring of 1849 Mr. Thomas Butler King had been sent as secret
agent of the government to California to acquire the fullest possible information

The coming convention was now the one theme of discussion, so far indeed as all political discussion was not lost in the gold excitement. For the few intervening months before its assembling, the Mexican system of law must be put in operation. In order that it might be known, as well as possible, what the law really was, a translation and digest of such portions of the Mexican laws as were supposed to be still in force, was prepared by Secretary Halleck and Translator Hartnell, and three hundred copies were, on July 2, ordered for distribution among the officers.* In the South this worked naturally, but it was decidedly awkward in the towns and among the miners of the North. As a mere temporary arrangement while the country was being flooded with immigrants, it gave moderate satisfaction.†

The Constitutional Convention was at hand; this tardy digest excited little popular attention; few but lawyers cared to antagonize it. Complaints and pessimism were passing away; the glittering prospect of the new régime now at last amounted to assurance; it may almost be said to have been ushered in antecedently to the one event which made it actual,—namely, the making of the constitution.

ROCKWELL D. HUNT.

University of the Pacific.

and to urge the people to give themselves a state constitution that they might petition Congress for admission into the union. "California Message and Correspondence," pp. 9-11. King arrived in California at the time when General Riley's proclamations were being issued. Here we come upon one of the happiest coincidences of California's history. The leading settlers of the territory loyally acquiesced in the *de facto* governor's plans, which also were thus approved by anticipation in Washington (instructions dated April 3), for Riley had resolved on calling a convention of the people's representatives before the arrival of King.

* This digest is in Browne's "Debates," app. xxiv et seq.

† Willey, in *Overland Monthly*, Vol. ix, p. 15.

ARGONAUTS OF CALIFORNIA

THE ARRIVAL IN SAN FRANCISCO—GOLD MACHINES—GOING TO THE
    MINES—THE BULLWHACKER—ARRIVAL IN HANGTOWN—THE
    VIEW FROM THE HILL.

THE city presented the appearance of a vast army encampment, and it was evident that the advance guard of Alexander's army had arrived sure enough, and had conquered what they sought. In the contemplation of the scene as we saw it from the roof of the cook's galley, we found deep consolation in the thought that in case the future would prove that we had travelled so many thousands of miles in search for gold, only to find upon our arrival that we had been badly sold, we were not alone at any rate. There was a grim satisfaction, therefore, in viewing the great number of vessels at anchor in the harbor from the various ports of the world, that had brought to the coast thousands of others for the same purpose.

Our voyage being ended upon our arrival in California, it is now, after upwards of forty years have passed since we sailed in through the Golden Gate, of some interest to know what has become of the passengers and crew of the old ship, and in fact of the ship also. The ship, after returning again to New Bedford, was fitted out for a whaling voyage and lost, I think in an ice pack in the Arctic Ocean. Captain Seabury, after serving for several years as master of a China steamer in the employ of the Pacific Mail Co., and also upon the Atlantic coast from New York to Aspinwall, a few years since retired from active service, and now lives in ease and comfort at his home in New Bedford. Of the passengers, there are but three of us at present remaining upon the Pacific Coast. Many of them died here. The greater portion of them returned to their Eastern homes; but a few of them are now left, and of all that number of gold hunters, not one of them succeeded in his anticipations of filling a pork barrel with the precious metal and but a small portion of them in filling an old boot-leg, or a beer-bottle, with the same.

It is necessary to explain here, that the ingenuity of many mechanics in the far-off Atlantic States had been exercised in the construction of various devices for the extraction of gold from the sand and soil which were, unfortunately, mixed with it. Our passengers, having full faith in their great value and efficacy, had brought quite a number of such machines with them. They were of all varieties and patterns; made of copper, iron, zinc and brass. Some of them were to be worked by a crank; others, more pretentious, having two cranks; whilst another patent gold washer, more economical and efficient, worked with a treadle. One variety was upright, requiring the miner to stand while using it. Still another, the inventor of which being of a more benevolent and humane temperament, was arranged in such a manner that the poor tired miner could sit in his arm-chair and take his comfort as he worked it.

One machine requires special mention. It was in the shape of a huge fanning mill, with sieves properly arranged for assorting the gold ready for bottling. All chunks too large for the bottle would be consigned to the pork barrel. This immense machine which, during our passage, excited the envy and jealously of all who had not the means and opportunity of securing a similar one, required of course the services of a hired man to turn the crank, whilst the proprietor would be busily engaged in shovelling in the pay dirt and pumping water; the greater portion of the time, however, being required, as was firmly believed in the corking of the bottles and fitting heads to the pork barrels. This machine was owned by a Mr. Allen, from Cambridge, Mass., who brought with him from that renowned head-center of learning, a colored servant who was to manage and control the crank portion of the invaluable institution; and so sanguine were all passengers in regard to the nature and value of the various machines for the purposes of saving, or for the extraction of gold, that apparently nothing but actual trial could convince them to the contrary.

Their faith in all kinds of mining machinery was put to the test sooner than expected; for upon landing, we found lying upon the sand and half buried in the mud, hundreds of similar machines, bearing silent witness at once to the value of our gold-saving machinery, without the necessity of a trial. Of course ours were also deposited carefully and tenderly upon the sandy beach, from

where, in a short time, they were washed into deep water, making amusement for the shrimps, clams, and crabs, which were no doubt under the impression that some unfortunate Italian vessel, with a cargo of hand-organs, had foundered in the locality. It was reported soon after, that the crew of a Dutch vessel that passed near Rincon Rock close by one dark and foggy night, saw distinctly a group of sea nymphs seated upon it, and that each one of them was engaged in turning the crank of what appeared to be some kind of a musical instrument. Old Neptune was seen standing in their midst as leader of the orchestra, keeping time with his sluice fork.

We saw scattered around among the bushes near the shore, also, a great number of trunks, chests, and valises of all sizes, and the most of them containing clothing of all descriptions, in many cases of value. These had all been thrown aside as useless encumbrances by their owners, who had started for the mines, being unable to pay the extra freight charged upon them.

We found that no wharves had yet been constructed, and the tide being out, it was somewhat difficult to land without wallowing through a short distance of very dark mud.

One of the sights which attracted our attention was a newly-constructed sidewalk, commencing at the building at that time occupied by Simmons, Hutchinson & Co., and extending in the direction of Adams & Co's. express office, for a distance of about seventy-five yards, I think. In any other portion of the earth except California, this sidewalk would have been considered a very extravagant piece of work, hardly excelled by the golden pavements in the new Jerusalem. The first portion of the walk was constructed of Chilean flour, in one hundred pound sacks, and which in one place had been pressed down nearly out of sight in the soft mud. Then followed a long row of large cooking stoves, over which it was necessary to carefully pick your way, as some of the covers had been accidentally thrown off. Beyond these again, and which completed the walk, was a double row of boxes of tobacco, of large size. Although this style of walk may seem very extravagant, even to an old pioneer, yet at that time sacks of Chilean flour, cooking stoves, tobacco, and pianos were the cheapest materials to be found, for lumber was in the greatest demand, selling in some instances at $600 per M., whilst the former articles, in consequence of the great supply, were of little value.

The town presented a strange scene. There were but few buildings; but the surrounding hills were covered with tents scattered promiscuously about, without regard to method or order.

Business of all kinds was lively, and although coin was scarce, yet gold dust answered every purpose.

Gambling houses and bar-rooms were numerous for the accommodation of citizens ; but the former, for the accomodation, more especially, of the miners, who were daily arriving from the mines, and who could be seen coming from the landing place toward Adams & Co.'s express office with their sacks of gold dust, to be sold or forwarded to their friends in the East. Many, however, were forced to return again to the mines in a few days, after having struck bedrock in one of the gambling houses, in their curiosity to discover upon which end of the tiger its tail was hung; and they generally made the discovery.

We found the cost of living in the city very high, although certain articles, as flour, for instance, were plentiful and cheap. Meals at the restaurants were from one to two dollars. One of our passengers had about 8o pounds of sweet potatoes, which he sold readily for one dollar per pound, and also a few orangers which he sold for one dollar each.

The following bill of fare gives an idea of the cost of living:

BILL OF FARE.—WARD HOUSE.

RUSSEL & MYERS　　　-　　　　-　　　　-　　　　PROPRIETORS.

San Francisco, Thursday, October 27, 1849.

SOUP.

Ox Tail, ... $1 00

FISH.

Baked Trout, White and Anchovy Sauce, . . . $1 50

ROAST.

| Beef, . . . | $1 00 | Mutton Stuffed, . . | $1 00 |
| Lamb, stuffed, . . | 1 00 | Pork, Apple Sauce, . | 1 25 |

BOILED.

Leg Mutton, Caper Sauce . $1 25 | Corned Beef and Cabbage, $1 25
Ham, . . . $1 00

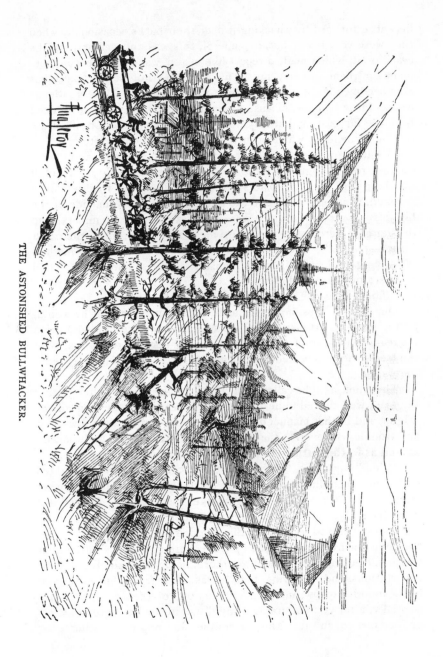

THE ASTONISHED BULLWHACKER.

his cattle forward by whacking it over their backs occasionally when they were very tired; but, in general, this was unnecessary, for the crack of it, which made a report like a gun, was a sufficient induce-ment for them to hurry up. This rare breed of bullwhackers has now become almost entirely extinct in California. More gentle, as well as more humane, means of driving cattle have been introduced from the far east, and it may not be out of place here to illustrate this by an incident which occurred only a few months later.

A bullwhacker, with his four yoke of cattle, was driving up over the hill from Hangtown, on his way to Sacramento City. The hill was long and in some places quite steep, and the road was very crooked, winding among and around the trees. On the side of the hill was a log cabin in which were living a company of miners from the State of Vermont. The ox driver stopped in front of the cabin for a rest, and the Vermonters laughed at and ridiculed his method of driving cattle with such a monster whip, used in such a cruel manner; but Pike said that:

" Them air cattle couldn't be driv any other way."

One of the boys, however, made a bet with him that he would, by the use of a little switch only, sit in the empty wagon and drive his team to the top of the hill, without accident or running against the trees. Pike accepted the bet, and with the rest of them got into the wagon.

The Yank, as Pike called him, cut a light switch, and after getting the oxen well started under way, took his seat upon the front of the wagon, and in that manner drove them to the top of the hill without any trouble whatever, to the great astonishment of the bullwhacker, as well as to the cattle too, no doubt.

" Well," says Pike, "if that don't beat anything I ever heerd tell on. I hev seen um drive a heap of cattle in old Missouri, but never seen it done with a little baby gad like that before. Blamed if I don't try it myself; you Yanks beat thunder."

I have neglected to mention that, before leaving Sacramento for the mines, many who had been up there were now returning on their way home again, if they could get there, being disappointed in their expectations, and declaring that it was all a fraud, but little gold being found anyhow, and then only, as one of them told me confi-dentially, after you had to dig away down in the hard ground three or four feet to find it. This, of course, was not very encouraging

news for men who had sailed around Cape Horn, and then to find
that it was all a fraud; but we started on, however, as before stated,
for the mines.

We passed many on their way down who had become discour-
aged and homesick. Among them were two or three acquaintances
of mine who had been into the mines about two weeks, and were
now returning to the East. They explained the state of affairs, say-
ing that there was but little gold to be found, and that it required
very hard and laborious work in the hot sun to get it, and very dirty
work, too, as it was away down out of sight in the mud. They,
therefore, advised all acquaintances whom they met to return with
them.

We concluded, however, to continue on and see with our own
eyes what the chances were, and if these men who were on the way
home had really spoken the truth. It required many years to find
this out; and if the great majority of miners who are now mining,
and others who mined many long years, were asked their opinion
in relation to it, they would be unanimous in their conclusion that
these men did come near telling the truth, although unconscious of
the fact at the time.

It seems to have been the opinion of many who came into California soon after the discovery of gold, that the rich metal was to
be found upon the surface of the ground, and that it could be very
easily scraped up and cleaned from the dirt. Consequently, there
was much disappointment upon finding that it was necessary to dig
in the mud and water for it. When engaged in mining, soon after,
near the road many emigrants who had crossed the plains with their
ox teams would stop alongside of the road and watch the process of
mining. -Upon one occasion an emigrant inquired:

" Wall, now, and is thet the way you fellers hes to do to get the
derned stuff?"

When informed that such was the method necessary to get it, he
remarked:

" Yas; well, then, I don't keer for none in mine. Gee haw, buck,
jest go lang thar!"

And for this reason hundreds passed through the mining region
to the valleys below.

About noon of the fourth day from Sacramento we crossed over
the hill, from the summit of which the town, with its log cabins and

tents, was visible below.   We descended to near the foot of the hill, where we unloaded our effects among a cluster of pines.   From this point we had a full view of the creek and portions of the various ravines, where we saw hundreds of busy men hard at work with pick

"DON'T WANT NONE IN MINE."

and shovel.   From the busy scene a spectator, who was unaware of the object of this laborious work, would imagine that an army had encamped in the locality and were at work in the trenches.

My native town was well represented, there being at this time about three hundred there from New Bedford who had sailed around the Horn. I found many acquaintances among them, and all appeared to be cheerful and confident of success in their new business. I should judge, after looking about and among the various flats,

THE DANDY MINERS.

creeks, ravines and gulches for a few days, that at this time there were about four thousand persons altogether in town and in the immediate vicinity, but only about half of them, however, were engaged in mining. The latter class was composed, at this early day, almost entirely of citizens of the United States, although there were a few from other countries, and all kinds of trades and professions were represented.

Here at work in the mud and water, with his gold spectacles and kid gloves, was a lawyer. Near him was a physician with his pants in his boots, sporting a plug hat. Here could be found clerks, bankers, storekeepers, barbers, hotel waiters, sea captains and mates, hotel-keepers and congressmen, nearly all from the New England States, who had come around Cape Horn to seek their fortunes.

Upon a slight elevation two well-dressed men were hard at work; they were lawyers from the city of New York, and were styled the dandy miners; they continued mining for several months and succeeded in making a very respectable fortune.

Upon the arrival of the first gold seekers in the summer and fall of '49, houses were, of course, unnecessary. Those who were fortunate enough to be the owners of tents occupied them, but the greater portion made their camps in the shade of the trees. As winter drew near, however, it was evident that other means of shelter would be necessary, consequently log cabins were constructed around among the ravines and gulches in all suitable localities convenient to a spring of water. Wood for fuel was, of course, plenty. Lumber for building purposes was scarce and very dear. All household furniture, such as chairs, tables, etc., was constructed in the most primitive style, often from old barrels and boxes when convenient.

Much ingenuity was displayed by various ones in the construction of these household necessities, but more especially in the case of chairs. The miner's easy chair, which he loved to take his comfort in after the work of the day was over, was usually made from an empty flour barrel, being cut out in the proper manner and made with rockers. Some, who possessed more aristocratic tendencies, would have these chairs lined and stuffed in good style, and they were pronounced very comfortable and equal to anything that could be bought in New York or Boston.

One remarkable fact was noticed at this early day in relation to the habits of the forty-niners, when we take into consideration their isolated condition, away from the influences of civilized society, and that was in the observance of the Sabbath, for, as a general rule, all Eastern men especially were true to their early training, and rested from their labor, or rather from their mining labors. It was upon this day that all mending and washing was done, and other little

THE MINERS AT HOME.

necessary household duties attended to, for it must be remembered that the washwoman had not put in an appearance yet, but she was, however, on the way.

On Sunday afternoons the clothes lines would be seen filled with a great assortment of woolen goods, socks, etc., the one thing need-

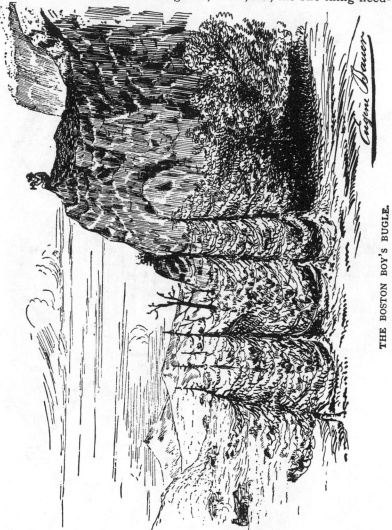

THE BOSTON BOY'S BUGLE.

ful to give all the appearance of a more advanced condition of civilization, however, was wanting, viz.: the "biled shirt," which came later, and was contemporaneous with woman.

As before mentioned, the chief amusement upon Sunday afternoons with the great majority was in lounging around the various saloons and gambling-houses; but to many, however, this part of the day was devoted to visiting the cabins of each other. There were many good singers to be found among the ravines and gulches, and upon pleasant moonlight evenings could be heard the notes of "Ben Bolt" from the boys who occupied the cabin on the hill above, while from another cabin in the ravine could be heard the refrain of "Do They Miss Me at Home," or "Sweet Home." Some, also, could be heard singing the songs we used to hear of, "Life on the Ocean Wave," "The Last Rose of Summer," or, perhaps, "Old Dan Tucker," all to be concluded by the singing of "Old Hundred," "Siloam," and "Coronation," and other tunes of a similar character.

There were also many good musicians to be found among the miners. Many of them had brought their instruments with them, and often at night could be heard echoing from the ravines and cañons the sounds of the fiddle, flute, accordeon and clarionet. One young man from Boston had brought with him his favorite instrument, the bugle, and when perched above upon the summit of a hill overlooking the town upon pleasant moonlight evenings, the strains of "Oft in the Stilly Night," "The Emigrant's Lament," or the martial strains of "The Red, White and Blue," or "The Star Spangled Banner," from his bugle, would be heard echoing far and near, among the ravines and gulches, and hailed by all with the greatest delight.

CHAPTER VI.

BUSINESS IN THE MINES—THE VARIOUS MINING CAMPS—PHYSICIANS
IN CAMP—DR. RANKIN—COLOMA—PROCESS OF MINING—THE
'49 EMIGRATION—SAUERKRAUT—FEMALE INFLUENCE ILLUS-
TRATED.

WE found on arriving in Hangtown quite a number of business
houses, stocked with a very good assortment of provisions
and nearly all other articles for miner's use.   The merchants, as well
as I can remember, were Thomas & Young; W. T. Coleman; Say-
ward & Thorndike; Judge Russel; Mr. Job; Judge Daniells; C.
Williams, while a short distance above upon the bank of the creek
were the stores of Frost, Brewster & Price, and just below town was
the store of the Governor.

There were three hotels in town: one large log-cabin, used for
a hotel, was called the Eldorado, and owned by Mr. Eltsner; another
one was kept by J. Adams, and the third by Col. Backus.   The most
numerous business houses in town were, however, the saloons and
gambling houses.

At Cold Springs, a few miles below Hangtown, was located a
mining camp, at this time consisting of a cluster of tents used for
saloons and for gambling houses, and one provision store, owned by
Burgess & Hill.

On the road towards Coloma, at the mining camp called Kelsy,
named after the man who discovered the placer mines here, were
also two stores with the usual complement of saloons.   At Coloma,
which is situated upon the South Fork of the American River, we
found a number of stores and saloons, whilst just below this camp
were the old saw mill and tail rate, where Marshall found the nug-
get of gold which has been the means of revolutionizing society and
changing social conditions among us, as well as settling up the whole
Pacific coast in so short a space of time.

Across the river could also be seen at this time, the name of

John T. Little in large letters, on the side of an extensive ware-house. This, with other various signs, informed the mining community that here could be found all kinds of mining supplies, and that the highest price was paid for gold dust. Following the road past Mr. Little's store, up over the mountain towards the middle fork of the American River, we found several camps where rich mines had been discovered. At Coloma down towards the old mill was the store of Shannon & Cady, and near to this were the stores of Perkins & Co., Tailor & Co., and also the gun and ammunition store of F. Beckhart. Of the business men, there are now living Thomas & Young; W. T. Coleman, Mr Darlington, who is at the present time in business at Placerville; Mr. Thorndike; Judge Russell; Mr. Caples; Mr. Price, and I think, Mr. Brewster, all of Hangtown. Mr. J. T. Little and Mr. Beckhart are both residing at the present time also in San Francisco, and no doubt many of the early business men are yet living in the East, or in some remote corner of the earth.

Of the physicians who were residing in the mining regions at this early day, a number of them are yet living; and as far as I know these are Dr. Bacon of Coloma; Dr. Clark, who is now residing at Stockton; Dr. Worthen, and I was informed that Dr. Ober is at the present time living east of the Rockies. We found also in the town five or six physicians, among the most prominent of whom were Dr. Wakefield, Dr. Kunkler, Dr. Ober, and Dr. Worthen, who is at the present time engaged in his profession and residing in the same old locality. There were Dr. Rankin, also, who had an extensive practice, and Dr. Clark.

In connection witn Dr. Rankin, an amusing incident which occurred in the fall of '49 may not be out of place here. The doctor was a Southerner by birth, and one of the old school, as his style of dress, which consisted of a white fur plug hat, blue coat with brass buttons, a buff-colored vest with trowsers to match, indicated. Upon certain occasions he sported a frill shirt front as well. Dressed in this style, he went one day astride his favorite Bucephalus, to visit a patient a few miles from town. It had been raining recently, and the road upon which he was travelling was house deep with soft yellow mud. He passed on his way a tall, large, raw-boned Scotchman, carrying upon his shoulder a sack of flour, and as he passed the pedestrian the doctor remarked that wallowing through the deep mud with a load like that must be tough work.

"Well," retorted the Scotchman, "and that's me ain business; and hed I ye doon here, me mon, I wad wallow ye in the mud, too."

"You would, would you," says the doctor, at the same time

HE DONE IT WEEL.

leaping from his horse, and landing knee-deep in the mud alongside of the Scotchman.

The latter laid down his burden upon a log, and seizing the doctor by the nape of the neck and seat of his pants, he raised him up and dropped him in the deepest part of a mud-hole. The doctor wasn't long in getting out, and mounting his horse was soon on his way home, remarking to the valiant Scot as he turned to leave:

"Well, now, Scotty, you done that weel."

"It was about sixteen years afterwards that the doctor was sitting in the bar-room of the What Cheer House, in Sacramento City, and in company with a few others, talking of old times. During the conversation he related how the tall Scotchman had rolled him in the yellow mud, and how he looked as though he had been run through a miner's ground sluice. Sitting tipped back in a chair at the side of the room was an old farmer, half asleep, but listening very attentively to the reminiscences of old times. When the doctor commenced relating the incident as above, the old farmer raised upon his feet, and at the conclusion stepped up, and placing his hand upon the Doctor's shoulder, remarked:

"Yas, doc', and ye told me, ye remember, that I doon it weel, too."

Of course the doctor was somewhat astonished, as well as pleased also, to meet his old antagonist, and again acknowledge once more that he doon it weel at any rate.

Handshaking and the usual refreshments followed, as a matter of course.

The town, or village, of Coloma, is situated upon the south branch of the American River; it was here that gold was first found by Marshall; the old mill where he worked is still standing. Mr. Marshall resided here during his life, living in a small cabin upon the side hill, a portion of which he had planted with vines and fruit trees. The first mining, of course, was done here, and this location constituted the germ or nucleus from which radiated all other mining localities, for it was from this point that the prospectors started out in various directions in the search for other mines. Some of the prospectors took a southerly course and found the rich deposits among the ravines of what is now called Hangtown creek. Others found Kelsey's, Spanish dry diggings, and further north they ran afoul of Georgetown and Greenwood, each locality deriving its name, when found, from some circumstance, event, or from the name of the finder. By the time of the arrival of the first gold seekers, who came via Cape Horn, hundreds of new locations had been made and named around the immediate vicinity of Coloma, and by the 1st of December, '49 the country had been traveled over and prospected, from Coloma to the Slanislau River on the south, and up to the Yuba River on the north, and valuable mines found for over a hundred miles in both directions.

Before commencing the business of mining, our little company concluded first to build a residence, which we constructed of logs in the regulation style, with chimney in the rear, the front door opposite, and after stowing away pots, pans and kettles in their proper places, putting up bunks with all the neccessary arrangements of curtains, out-riggers, etc., a few more blows with the hammer here and there made us master of the situation, or of the castle, at least.

After finishing our residence, we started in to the business of mining, for which we had traveled nearly half way around the globe. In a large ravine near at hand, called Oregon Ravine, as it was first found by a man from that State, we determined to make our first effort. There were at work in the same locality about two hundred others. The method of mining was of the most primitive character. The dirt would be dug down to the bed-rock and thrown to one side, as the dirt and gravel in immediate contact with the bed-rock, including the surface of the latter also, was all that was considered of any value. This was put into sacks and packed upon our backs down to the creek, where the gold was separated from it by panning. Many, however, would spread their pay dirt upon the ground, and when it was thoroughly dry would winnow it out by pouring it from the pan to the ground, the wind, when strong enough, answering a very good purpose. This was the style of mining as practiced by the Mexicans and also the Chileans, but it was a very slow process, and would only pay when no water could be found.

From the hill above, it was a strange sight to see men of all classes and from every State in the Union thus clustered together upon one spot in common, and all inspired with the one desire, i. e., to dig gold. All hard at work in the mud and water, with pick and shovel, each one determined to do his level best to get all he could in the shortest time possible.

Over in that ravine yonder is a crowd of Yankees from Maine and Vermont, with a leavening of a few Missourians and Kentuckians. In that large ravine to the right are three or four hundred hard-working, earnest, gold seekers from Massachusetts and New

HANGTOWN IN '49.

C.W. HASKINS

York, and from Connecticut and Ohio, as well as a few from Georgia, Arkansas and Old Virginia. Upon that extensive flat below, the great crowd at work is of a more cosmopolitan character, being composed of men from all States in nearly equal proportions. But few are noticed at present hailing from the Southern States, except those of a sporting character, who will be found among the saloons and gambling houses. Among these, a few of the old style Southern politicians, who are dressed in regulation blue dress-coat, with its great brass buttons, and a white plug hat, can be seen daily promenading around from place to place, with the crooked cane hanging upon the arm. The emigration across the plains in the fall of 1849 was estimated to be about 25,000. But a small proportion of them, however, remained in the mining regions. The greater number of them being farmers, passed through to make their homes in the valleys below.

Much has been said and written in relation to the arrival of the first young ladies in the mines; but the very first young ladies who made their appearance in the mining regions of California arrived at this time. They were the daughters of Mrs. Stuart, from the State of Illinois. Their father died during the journey across the plains. They arrived in Hangtown about the middle of September, returning again to their Eastern homes sometime during the summer or autumn of '50.

There were many women and children in the emigration of this season, and in consequence of the scarcity of feed for the teams, many of them were compelled to trudge along through the sandy desert and over the steep and rough mountain roads, for hundreds of miles.

One family to arrive at this time was that of Dr. Kunkler, with his wife and son, who was about six years of age, and an incident in relation to them is worthy of record. An accident happened to the doctor through which he was unable to travel on foot, and was consequently obliged to ride in the wagon. They were traveling with an ox-teem, and for this reason, the accident to him was very unfortunate, since it was absolutely necessary for one of the party to walk alongside of the team for a part of the time, especially when traveling among the hills. Mrs. Kunkler was a French lady, and born in the city of Paris. She was of slight build, delicate in appearance, and unaccustomed to such hardships; but it was now absolutely necessary that she should take charge of the ox team, for a time at least. All emigrants who cross the plains are well aware that this is a very difficult duty to perform, even for a man. To attend to and hunt the cattle, cook and wait upon the sick and the children also, and to make ready for a start again—all of this the delicate French lady attended to in good style, and walked alongside of her team (for over 800 miles) which she managed like a veteran,

"DIS AM A FREE KENTRY, MASSA."

arriving in Hangtown in August, '49, in the best of health and spirits.

The doctor and his wife have both crossed to the other side; but the son, having inherited the profession of the father, practiced in San Francisco until a short time ago, when he also joined the great majority.

Quite a number of slaves from Tennessee and Kentucky were brought across the plains during this year, and were taken into the mines by their masters. This kind of mining by slave labor did not, however, prove a success, and was soon abandoned. One man from Tennessee, brought his slaves, three in number, into Hang-town and located in a small gulch near Spanish Ravine. The claim which they worked was rich, and the master was happy, although his happiness was of short duration, for he was very much aston-ished at the close of one very pleasant day, when, as he went to take possession of the gold dust which had been washed out during the day, he was politely informed by his rebellious subjects to " Jess take his hands off from dat ar gold dust, as it belonged to dem."

He was further informed that " Dey was now in a free country and slaves no mor'; but if Massa was willin' to come in and work with 'em on sheers he could do so."

He endeavored to reason with the boys, but in vain. He told them that he would appeal to the law, which he finally did; but with no better success, and he returned in disgust to Tennessee leaving his slaves masters of the field, as well as of themselves.

Two slaves worked in the Spring of '50 in Log Cabin Ravine, now Bedford ave. They were from the city of Louisville, Ky., and owned by a very prominent physician at that place. The doctor had furnished his two slaves with a good team and all necessary supplies, and had sent them forth to earn their freedom, the agree-ment being that when they had forwarded to him the sum of twenty-three hundred dollars in gold, the master in return would send them their " freedom papers." They were informed that they were free men, and it was unnecessary to send money to purchase their freedom; but they were firm in their purpose to do just as they had agreed with their master, and since he had trusted in their word they should not disappoint him, and they did not. The money was sent to their master through Adams & Co.'s Express, and in due time they received their papers. In a few months afterwards they forwarded to their late master the sum of eight hundred dol-lars also, as the price of their sister's freedom, and in the fall of '50 the met her brothers in Hangtown with her papers of deliverance in her pocket.

There were no cradles or toms at this time in the mines, for the reason that there was no water; but with the first rains, cradles made their appearance, and towards Spring long toms were used, but regular sluices did not come into use until a year later. The first hole that we dug after having measured off and staked our claims, fifteen feet square to each man, in accordance with the miners' law, gave us the gold very fine, and by the advice of a few veteran miners who had followed the business off and on for nearly eight days, we moved to other vacant spots nearer to the center of the ravine (Oregon Ravine), where we found the gold much coarser and easier to save. It was the custom for miners to get out to work as early in the morning as possible, usually about eight o'clock, and we quit work about four P.M. This gave us sufficient time to finish our evening meal, and to dress up, ready for a long evening, lounging through the various gambling houses and seeing the sights in town, which, however, at this early day were not to be compared in number or in gorgeousness with those of a year later. The chief pleasure, however, among us was in visiting the cabins of each other, and listening to the old yarns from the seafaring men, or in tasting of some of their favorite dishes, which they had learned to manufacture out on the ocean; such for instance as " dundefunk," " lobsconce," and a variety of others; to hear the various opinions expressed upon the subject of cooking. It gave us the impression that cooking was one of the fine arts, and that the only object in life or the chief aim in existence was to eat. Of course we, the novices in the art, soon became quite expert in the chemical combination necessary for dundefunk, lobsconce, hard and soft tack, etc., and in a short time were able to boast of our dexterity, also, in whirling a flapjack up through the chimney and catching it again in our frying pan, right side up, by holding the latter out doors on the other side of the house.

It was customary, also, among many of the miners to play all kinds of practical jokes upon each other, and one amusement, in particular, was to place a flat stone, or board, upon the top of a chimney, and then to be near at hand in the morning when the victims were trying to cook their breakfast amidst the smoke, occasionally coming to the door with the tears streaming down their cheeks, swearing until all nature around looked blue. They would assert that some " infernal sea cook " had come in the night and stolen the draught, or had turned the chimney "tother end up." It didn't take long, however, to discover the cause, and then the remark was "that Nantucket sea cook of a Tom Ferney done it," they knew.

It is necessary to explain here, as it may be the means of giving a wrong impression in relation to the habits of the old-timers, to elucidate what is meant by the boys dressing up after the day's work was done. In all civilized societies the expression "to dress up" signifies to change, or to alter one's general appearance by the donning of "a biled shirt," store clothes and a plug hat, perhaps.

SMOKED OUT.

There was no necessity, however, in the mines tor being very particular about the style. It is true that at this time there would be found occasionally one who would shave or trim up his whiskers and even don a fancy necktie, but he was looked upon with suspicion.

His ancestors were sporting men, probably, and he had inherited the tendency. There was not, in the opinion of these old-timers, any necessity or use in dressing up in "store clothes" or "biled shirts." The "dress up," therefore, to which I had reference, consisted of washing the face and hands, taking a fresh cud of fine cut (Mrs. Miller's brand), or donning a clay pipe, well stocked.

All of my readers, perhaps, have during their lives many times read of or heard discussed the old worn-out subject of "female influence," but it is but very seldom that any of us are enabled to see the effect of the *absence* of woman so practically illustrated as it was in the mines. For the first two years, or up to the arrival of the emigration from across the plains in the fall of '50, the condition of the mining population, especially their carelessness in regard to appearances, mode of life, and habits in general, showed conclusively that man, when alone, and deprived of that influence which the presence of woman only can produce, would in a short time degenerate into a savage and barbarous state.

At this time, also, there was but little necessity for law, except to restrain the vicious element among the few Mexican horse-thieves, who had found their way into the mining regions, but this class, Judge Lynch dealt with in a very summary style, and they soon became scarce. No standing army or armed force of policemen were required to protect the rights of the forty-niners, for they were, as a general rule, a class who respected law and order, as well as the rights of others, and illustrated the fact that among a class of men who are disposed to do what is right, with no desire to injure or trespass upon the rights of others, no law for their government or control is really necessary. It is very true, however, that in the cases of many who had occupied high positions in church organizations in the East, upon finding themselves thus placed, afar from all restraint and church influences, did reveal their true nature by falling from grace and practicing habits that were strictly prohibited by ecclesiastical law. Yet these were the exceptions, only; not the rule. We were, of course, under the jurisdiction of the U. S. Government; but no laws could be put into force or executed as no officers had been appointed for the purpose. We elected, however, an Alcalde, according to the Mexican custom, who decided all cases occurring in relation to the disputes among miners. All cases of a criminal nature were decided by a committee of the whole, a jury for the purpose being chosen from the mining community, and all criminals being granted a fair and impartial trial.

But a change soon took place in our political affairs, for upon November 13th, 1849, the constitution of the Territory was adopted, and Peter H. Burnett was elected our first Governor.

The election to vote upon the adoption of the constitution and for Governor in this portion of the mining region was held in the hotel of Col. Bachus, Hangtown, and the border element was very strongly opposed to the whole business, claiming that we did not require law and order, constitution or Governor either; that we were getting along well enough without them ; if the Yanks undertook to play any sich nonsense they would be sorry for it ; they made some show of resistance, but when they saw that the Yanks were in dead earnest, and had come to the place of voting well armed and prepared to maintain law and order, they very reluctantly departed in disgust and the constitution was adopted unanimously.

The first persons hung in California subsequent to the gold discovery, were two Mexicans and an American. They were hung for horse stealing and robbery during the fall of '48, in Hangtown, and it was from this fact that the mining camp derived its name, and although the camp has enjoyed the unenviable reputation of being the place where many murderers and horse-thieves have been kindly laid to rest by the citizens, in committees of the whole, yet only one other individual was ever hung by the citizens of the place, and that was Irish Dick, a young gambler, who was executed in the fall of '50 for murder. A jury, composed of miners, was chosen ; he was granted a fair trial, declared guilty, and sentenced to be hung from the old oak tree which stood upon the side of the hill across the creek, at 2 P. M. of the same day. He requested permission to leap from the limb of the tree, head foremost ; but this favor, of course, could not be granted since it did not conform to the law, and would be a very barbarous proceeding, as well as a bad precedent to establish, for in some parts of the country the trees were very small.

The first rainstorm in the fall of '49 occurred October 13th. It was a shower lasting but a few hours, and continuing in this manner throughout the winter months with light showers, but enough, however, for the working of cradles; and now was inaugurated the process of mining in a more business-like and profitable manner.

Claims, which by the panning process yielded daily but an ounce or
so, now gave down, by the use of the cradle, from one to ten

LAW AND ORDER TRIUMPHANT.

ounces, and in some cases even double the last amount. The rich-
est part of any ravine or gulch, was, of course, near the center, or

where the water course had deposited the greatest quantity, consequently the first miners would confine their work chiefly to such portions of a ravine, and those who came after would work nearer the banks, where the gold was usually finer and much lighter. By the use of this machine very high wages could be made from gravel, which would not pay to pan.

As winter approached, emigrants who had come by steamer and across the Isthmus of Panama, as well as " around the Horn," now commenced to arrive in great numbers, and not being satisfied with the prospects of the camp scattered about in various directions over the country in the search for new mines. Soon other towns and camps were started ; some very rich and valuable placer mines being discovered in the vicinity of Hangtown. Great excitement prevailed, and at this period of its history Hangtown contained almost as large a population as the chief city of the country, San Francisco, and a year later Eldorado was called the banner county. The winter following passed without the occurrence of any events in this portion of the country worth relating. The rains were light, with but little snow, and the weather wa m. Towards spring news was received that rich mines had been found farther north. From this fact it was concluded that all the gold had originally been washed down from the north by floods or brought down by glacial action ; consequently, the mines would be richer as you advanced toward the North Pole. This belief was almost universal among the mining classes, and some were so sanguine that such would prove to be the case, that one miner offered to bet, "that if yer'd only go fur enough to the north yer'd find ther gold all coined and sacked up, ready for shipping." Great preparations were therefore made for leaving the old worked-out mining regions in the central portions of the State, and towards the spring of '50 the stampede commenced for the Yuba, Bear River, and other rich mining camps at the north.

BIBLIOGRAPHY

Hubert H. Bancroft, *History of California* (San Francisco, 7 vol., 1884-90)

Walton Bean, *California: An Interpretive History* (New York, 1968)

Robert G. Cleland, *Cattle on a Thousand Hills: Southern California, 1850-1880* (San Marino, 1951)

---- *From Wilderness to Empire* (New York, 1959)

Glenn S. Dumke, *The Boom of the Eighties in Southern California* (San Marino, 1944)

Omer Englebert, *Last of the Conquistadores: Junipero Serra* (New York, 1956)

Norman A. Graebner, *Empire on the Pacific* (New York, 1955)

Rodman W. Paul, *California Gold: The Beginning of Mining in the Far West* (Cambridge, Mass., 1947)

Ralph J. Roske, *Everyman's Eden: A History of California* (New York, 1968)

NAME INDEX

Alarcon, Hernando de, 1
Alvarado, Juan B., 6,7
Amador, Jose Maria, 12
Anza, Juan B. de, 2
Arguello, Luis A., 12

Bartlett, Washington, 16
Bigler, John, 11
Booth, Newton, 15
Brannan, Samuel, 8
Brown, Edmund G., 21,22
Bucareli, Viceroy, 2
Budd, James H., 17
Burnett, Peter H., 9,10

Cabrillo, Juan R., 1
Castanso, Miguel, 4
Castro, Manuel, 7
Charpenning, George, 11
Chavez, Cesar, 21, 22
Crespi, Father, 15

Dana, Richard H., 6
Diaz, Melchoir, 1
Downey, John G., 13
Dorr, Ebenezer, 4
Drake, Francis, 1

Echeandia, Jose M., 5,6
Engle, Claire, 21

Figueroa, Jose, 6
Fremont, John C., 7,8,14

Gage, Henry T., 17

Galvez, Jose de, 1
Gilbert, George S., 14
Gillett, James N., 18
Gilray, John, 5
Glenn, Hugh James, 17

Haight, Henry H., 15
Humboldt, Alexander von, 11

Irwin, William, 16

Johnson, Hiram W., 18
Johnson, J. Neely, 12
Jones, Thomas ap Catesby, 7

Kearny, Stephen W., 8
Kern, Edward M., 15
Knight, Goodwin J., 21

Laperouse, Comte de, 3
Lassen, Peter, 14
Latham, Milton, 13
Lincoln, Abraham, 14
Lopez, Francisco, 6
Low, Frederick F., 14

McDougal, John, 10
Markham, Henry H., 17
Marshall, James, 8
Mason, Richard B., 8
Merriam, Frank F., 19
Micheltorena, General, 7
Moraga, Gabriel, 17
Moraga, Jose J., 2
Muir, John, 17

117